PRAISE FOR *THE FIGHT OF YOUR LIFE*

Sexual integrity is vital to the covenant of marriage and *The Fight of Your Life* is chock-full of practical guidance for the man who is man enough to protect that covenant. Learn how to harness your God-given sexual desires. Stand up to sexual temptation and find God's power in your purity. Every man who is serious about his marriage will love this book. It's grounded, inspiring, and immeasurably practical.

DRS. LES AND LESLIE PARROTT
Authors of *Saving Your Marriage Before It Starts*

This book is an incredibly important call to arms for every man in today's culture! With wisdom and helpful detail, Tim and Mark unpack some vital information that men will want to know about a very common struggle, and provide not only the challenge to overcome it but the assurance that they can.

SHAUNTI FELDHAHN
Social researcher and best-selling author of
For Women Only and *Through A Man's Eyes*

From two men who have made indelible impressions on my own marriage comes a book that 97% of Christian marriages need desperately. (That's the percentage of godly marriages under the assault of pornography.) Tim and Mark marry biblical truth with scientific fact to create useable tools to win the battle.

DANNAH GRESH
Best-selling author and sexual theology teacher

In today's over-sexualized culture, sexual purity is more difficult than ever to attain. Tim Clinton and Mark Laaser are well aware of the devastation sexual sin causes in every facet of life. These men have put together a compelling guidebook on the effects of impurity and how to navigate a culture that flaunts sex at every turn. It is informative, insightful, and most of all: empowering!

JOE WHITE
Speaker, Author, and CEO

In *The Fight of Your Life* Dr. Tim Clinton and Dr. Mark Laaser tackle the topic of men and their sexuality head-on and provide a resource that is rigorous, both scientifically and biblically. It is rare to find such a blending of the two in a way that is so accessible and eminently helpful. If you are a man, I hope you will read this book and encourage your friends to do the same. I am confident you will be more like Jesus for having read this book.

ED STETZER
Executive Director of LifeWay Research,
author, conference speaker/leader, and pastor

THE
FIGHT
OF YOUR
LIFE

MANNING UP TO THE CHALLENGE OF SEXUAL INTEGRITY

TIM CLINTON & MARK LAASER

A Word of Caution

Because the topic of this book relates to sexual behaviors, we have worked hard to stay in the realm of fact and biblical principle, and at the same time to express scientific information and our beliefs as clearly and rationally as we can. However, we must still caution our readers against two possible temptations that may arise. When the topic is sex, there is always a danger that a person may find information titillating, or that a person who reads about the pervasive nature of sexual sin may feel a little "left out of the loop" and have a desire to do original research into the sin. We ask you to pray for strength in guarding yourself against both impulses as you move into the pages of this book.

DESTINY IMAGE® PUBLISHERS, INC.
P.O. Box 310, Shippensburg, PA 17257-0310
"Promoting Inspired Lives."

This book and all other Destiny Image and Destiny Image Fiction books are available at Christian bookstores and distributors worldwide.

Cover design by: Prodigy Pixel

For more information on foreign distributors, call 717-532-3040.
Or reach us on the Internet: www.destinyimage.com

ISBN 13: TP 978-0-7684-0699-3
ISBN 13 EBook: 978-0-7684-0700-6

For Worldwide Distribution, Printed in the U.S.A.
1 2 3 4 5 6 7 8 9 10 11 /18 17 16 15

CONTENTS

FOREWORD

There are no greater challenging or distressing topics in modern times than lust, pornography, and sex addiction. A tsunami-proportioned effect is yet to be realized in both the church and in society as a whole. The current statistics are absolutely staggering on how pornography has made its way into not only the individual lives of men but also now increasingly in the lives of women as well:

- 37% of all Internet traffic is pornography.

- 50% of churchgoing men admit a serious struggle with porn.

- 34% of churchgoing women have sought out online pornography.

- 54% of pastors admitted to viewing Internet porn in the past year and 30% admitted viewing within the past month.

Porn has become a modern-day aphrodisiac of choice for couples and is now being soaked up into the hearts of our children. The average age of first exposure has been cited as eleven and it creeps lower—many researchers are citing first exposure as young as eight years old. And these exposures are often happening as accidental discoveries in the home.

Very little is being said or done to address this elephant sitting in the pew of the church, in the living rooms of our homes, in our youth groups and Christian schools. I believe that if every parent, pastor, counselor and every person of influence understood the true danger we are facing, we would be that much closer to winning the battle against this perilous epidemic.

Sexual sin has been around since the beginning of time. The evil one has always used the natural sex drive gone wrong (or gone sinful) as a foothold of influence. There's something about sexual sin that is distinct from other sins. Paul talked about this type of sin as a sin against the body—and repeatedly shared the importance of living with sexual integrity. But with the advent of the Internet and the condition of our hearts, it truly is the fight of every man's life. Think with me what it would be like if men stood up and committed themselves to live free from the ties of sexual sin. Think about the ramifications and the gift it would be to future generations.

We are living in a different world than the generations before us. Our culture is being consumed by the lie that porn is healthy and improves sex; whereas we know that it ruins true intimacy. Porn ruins sex. It leaves all in its wake empty, isolated, and ashamed—certainly affected in some way.

I know firsthand the devastation of being on the receiving end of a sexual life that has gone awry. The abuse I suffered as a child went deep into my heart. I know that society needs this book not only for those struggling with pornography, but for those who stand to be impacted by the aggressive and oppressive changes pornography can bring with it.

We are living in a tumultuous time with thousands deeply hurting—but there is hope. There are answers. It's the grace of God that allows us to rise above it all.

In *The Fight of Your Life: Manning up to the Challenge of Sexual Integrity*, Drs. Clinton and Laaser do battle with this world and chart a course for freedom, integrity, and purity. This book could not have come at a better time. My prayer is that God would use *The Fight of Your Life* tenfold to bring glory to Himself and to allow men to know and understand what Paul said —it is for freedom, not bondage, that Christ has come to set us free (see Galatians 5:1).

What will the world look like if we, as men, take the call to "man up" and take this challenge seriously? Think of how many marriages will be saved! Think of how many sons will be rescued from the torturous bondage of sexual addiction. How many daughters will stand at the wedding altar free from concern over their new husband's history with pornography? How many churches and pastors will find new freedom in worship, no longer stifled by shame? The list goes on and on. It's time to stand.

I'm on my hands and knees right now asking God to bless each and every one who will encounter these pages, that God will set the hearts of men free. Without purity, there is no power. If you read and embrace the teaching in *The Fight of Your Life*, you will be armed to take back the power that was lost—and to help others do so. I can't wait to hear what God does through this book.

JOSH D. McDOWELL
Author/Speaker

ACKNOWLEDGMENTS

Every book is on a journey from the original idea to its final appearance on bookshelves. Along the way many people encourage the idea and contribute to its development. Both of us lead very busy professional lives and have many family activities. There is absolutely no way we would have written this book without the help of all those people.

Special thanks go to Max Davis. He is one of those writers in the tradition of the South, capable of poetic and pithy prose. We appreciate his use of story and metaphor to shape the character of this book. Most important, we give thanks for his ability to continually return to the truth of Scripture and its central message of God's love and grace.

Also on our writing team was Carter Featherston. We thank him for his attention to the practical application of sound medical and psychological principles throughout this book. Like Max, he loves God and hungers to understand biblical truth. Thank you to David Jenkins, Michele Worley, and Becca Tomas. Your thoughtful recommendations and enthusiasm for this book's content have been very encouraging.

A special thank you to Dina Jones, Erica Wright, Emily Boyles and our team at AACC for helping research, shape, and live in the details in this book.

We thank our wives, Julie and Debbie, extraordinary women of faith who continue to encourage us in our writing and work. They do so out of their love for God and for us. Both of them are also great writers and speakers. It is a powerful gift to have had their input along the way.

We write this book in large part for our sons. Tim's son Zach and son-in-law Ben, and Mark's sons Jon and Ben are young men who are in the thick of this fight, the fight of every young man's life. Let us not forget our daughters, Tim's daughter Megan and Mark's daughter, Sarah. This book is for all of the men in their lives including Sarah's sons, Daryl and Devon.

A special thanks to the team at Destiny Image and Curtis Wallace for having faith in this book and for catching the vision of this battle that all men face.

Mostly we thank God for His power and grace and for guiding all of us past the roadblocks that Satan has tried to throw in the way of this book.

1

THE FIGHT OF YOUR LIFE

*Let us make man in our image, after our likeness. And let
them have dominion over...all the earth.... And the man
and his wife were both naked and were not ashamed.*

—GENESIS 1:26; 2:25 (ESV)

And God made man....

Out of the dust of the ground He made him. Adam. A red-blooded male. Unique. The pinnacle of creation.

God also formed every beast of the field and every bird of the heavens and brought them to the man to see what he would call them. And whatever the man called every living creature, that was its name.

According to the Genesis account, God spent time with him and walked with him and gave him dominion over the fish of the sea and over the birds of the heavens and over the livestock and over all the earth and over every creeping thing that creeps on the earth.

The Bible says that God was pleased with all that He created and declared that it was good.

But almost in the same breath, God said that there is one thing that is not good: "It is not good that man be alone."

So God caused a deep sleep to come over him and out of the rib of man God created Her, Eve, a woman. The one who Adam said was "bone of my bone and flesh of my flesh." The one who would come alongside him and complement him, similar in that they both were made in the image of God, but completely different in that He created them male and female.

The beauty of this design was very purposeful. In Genesis 2:24-25, God's plan was for them to come together in deep devotion and commitment to and for one another. To fulfill and taste what it means to love and be loved. To be one flesh, naked and unashamed.

Have you ever wondered what it must have been like the first time Adam saw her? Kissed her? Touched her? Held her?

A gift from God, in all of her splendor.

In the innocence of the Garden, the Man and the Woman were free—there for one another in all their glory to express love in every way toward God and each other. Free to be fruitful and multiply and fill the earth.

FROM BEAUTY TO BROKENNESS

God made us to enjoy love and relationships, and to enjoy our sexuality in a loving marital relationship. As men, He made us to be aroused with the beauty of a woman and to enjoy her completely. It's natural. Amazing and wonderful.

There is nothing more wonderful than being in a relationship with someone you love who truly loves you. But there is also nothing more painful than being in a relationship with someone you love who doesn't truly love you.

And anything that has that much propensity for beauty also has that much propensity for pain.

You only have to read one chapter after Genesis 2 to move from beauty to brokenness. Anything that has that much beauty for God, anything that has that much beauty stamped on it by God, evil will want to destroy. When sin entered the Garden, it encroached on the intimacy between Adam and Eve, and their intimacy with God; it shattered that intimacy in pieces. Beauty turned to ashes. Intimacy turned to accusations. What was so beautiful and alluring became filled with shame and even painful.

Ever after, without intimacy, we human beings have been driven by our pain to find it.

And all of Hell knows this. When our lives and our relationships are not the way they are supposed to be and when God-ordained needs go unmet, we will turn to anything to fulfill the emptiness, the brokenness, the hole inside of us.

AND THE FIGHT IS ON...

The fight of our lives hits us before we even know what is happening. In the natural flow of life, when men hit puberty, testosterone starts flowing, and we feel a sexual drive in our bodies.

At first, the awakening of our sexual drive takes us by surprise. But soon even this area of our lives falls under the curse of competition between boys. Some of us mature faster and our bodies show the power of that. Some of us push aside discomfort about our interests and development through an awkward stage of youth. We wrestle with our identity and masculinity, stirred up by our sexual desires. Many feel embarrassed about it, and in the presence of others the embarrassment often turns to confusion and shame.

The new feelings impact our brains, our bodies, and our speech.

Girls begin to look different. Their hair. Their smile. Their smell. Their bodies. Their beauty. And as we take this all in, we learn a new vocabulary of words that demonstrates the electric charge we are starting to feel.

And for most men, this intensity doesn't let up much at all. Desire. Sexual energy. The battle for control. It's virtually every man's battle. It started with the natural progression of merely being a hormone-driven young boy, a youngster who has hit puberty. Then the fight grew more intense throughout junior high or middle school and on into high school. When that knockout girl stared at us, it created a fascination that locked in our brain for days. We stole lingering glances, and we noticed the beauty of her skin, and the softness of her face and neck. The smell of her hair as she passed by. Then we saw how soft and inviting her body was. She was captivating!

Sexual innuendos also came flying at us through the hormone-driven culture that we shared with our peers. The locker room was filled with stories of who was with whom last Friday night in the car. Did he touch her? Did she let him? How far did it go?

When we had our first taste of her lips, and we found out that many of these girls seemed just as interested as we were with the exploration of exhilaration. Our experiences were still more on the innocent side, but with these images up close, and our fantasies fueled with her profile pictures and smells of a young woman's beauty, we knew what it was now to feel that "burn," the burn Paul describes in First Corinthians 7:9 where he said, "It is better to marry than to burn." We couldn't have agreed more. She was fire and our desire grew. We knew what we wanted, and that it was the plan of God for us to have "Her" someday. We will definitely get married one day, we said. In the meantime, it was a fight. If we were not careful, our spiritual life and our sexual self would be diverging at lightning speed.

ENTER PORN

Many of us set out with intentions to stay within certain boundaries, and to keep ourselves under control. The burn, however, can become an all-consuming fire at a whole 'nother level. Gasoline gets thrown on the burning fire, usually through the world of pornography. Virtually every man can tell you the first time he saw pornography. It gets etched in the brain. And while abstinence is a wonderful, growing movement, research shows that most eventually cross the line with a woman. Perhaps it happens in high school, or in those college-age days. In 2013, the CDC reported that 46 percent of high schoolers had been sexually active.[1] Once it's lit, the burning fire can become a consuming fire, a total red zone.

One night with friends, a meaningless summer night with no agenda for evil, someone shows up with a pornographic magazine or DVD, or introduces you to a porn site. One date with a girl you don't know that well (but your friends say she was "hot") and you made moves or she seduced you into a sexual act that scandalized your heart. At your first job out of college, it might have happened when a slightly older woman was taken with your youthful good looks. You were drawn into a place that you never would've planned to go, but the power of hormones in the moment triggered your desire and changed your story.

Most live some ugly or painful memories of a path taken too far. The fight now is no longer merely about resisting temptations every day, but the fight has grown to include shame, fear, and even despair.

One look. One touch. One click too far, and you are drawn into a greater intensity in the fight of your life.

You may not be in the throes of sexual sin right now, but more than likely you have ruts and vulnerability in your heart, patterns of behaving that can keep your back door open to the enemy.

Every man is vulnerable to temptation. King David was described as "a man after God's own heart," yet his own heart went astray and committed adultery with Bathsheba. King Solomon was given unsurpassed wisdom by God, but even the wisest of men behaved foolishly when he gave in to his temptations. We read in First Kings 11:4 that, "As Solomon

---

1 From "Sexual Risk Behavior: HIV, STD, & Teen Pregnancy Prevention," on Centers for Disease Control and Prevention website (http://www.cdc.gov/healthyyouth/sexualbehaviors/) (Accessed February 5, 2015).

grew old, his wives turned his heart after other gods, and his heart was not fully devoted to the Lord his God, as the heart of David his father had been."

Today, the temptations are everywhere, especially online. You could be out on a date when a woman takes hold of you and leads you someplace you have never been before, or perhaps a place you had vowed to keep in your past, never to return to. You could get tempted next week by a casual relationship at work, and suddenly find yourself in trouble. Tonight, on your phone or the computer, you can hit the right sequence that will send an advertisement to the sidebar of your window, and the bell will toll! The fight is on!

We believe the sexual arena is one of the most glorious yet threatening dimensions of our lives. The Apostle Paul declared that sexual sin is against the body. It defiles you with the power to shame you, and you seemingly can't wipe it out of your mind. It's like getting hot tar on you. It burns until it cools and it's hard to wash off. It's hard to erase it from your conscience, and harder to scrub it out of your life.

We are going to explain to you why the fight is so intense, including the biological reasons for this intensity. We will tell you about your greatest sexual organ, and how God designed it. We will tell you how to break free and even tear down strongholds, and how to renew your mind. This is information that you must know if you are going to be faithful and true in the fight.

Maybe you or someone you know needs help and direction. We know the way to gain strength and power for the fight. Where there is no purity, there is no power; and where there is purity, power reigns. Christ has fought for our purity, and He has won that fight. You will be surprised as we talk candidly about how to live free. It's about grace. It's about His love. It's about walking with other men who want to fight, too. It's about truth and intimacy. We can't wait to show you what we've learned through the years as we have worked with thousands of men.

The pursuit of sexual integrity will present to you one of your greatest and most relentless challenges in life. The past ten to fifteen years have ramped it up and put this fight on steroids. We want you to be free. We want you to enjoy what God intended with the sexual life, to have that same Garden ecstasy when you "see Her" and marry her. When you touch, when you kiss, when you make love, as you live life with your wife, we want you to enjoy all God had in mind. If God gave you, as husband and wife, to one another, then you should enjoy it all! She is a gift. Sex is a gift.

Wherever God has called you in life, whether you are a pastor, a student, an athlete, a businessman, or pursuing your career, you have a unique calling from God. But we have seen the power of sex go awry, bringing men to their knees in defeat and discouragement and derailing men from their callings. We want to help you with the fight. We want to help you *win* in the fight. We want you to be able to enjoy the wife of your youth. We want to help you get back up and in the fight if you've been knocked down for the count.

If your heart still yearns for God to bring cleansing to your life then you have more hope for your struggle than you realize. Even if you have been on a hellish ride with your sexual struggle, we want you to know: God is still in the midst of your story. He has always been there. He is still at work. Though the gun barrels of Hell are aimed at you, the Lord Jesus Christ is warring with you. We do not fight alone. In His love He is saying, "We can make it. You work, and I'll work. Let's get this done together."

This fight is intimidating, but defeat and discouragement do not mean God has quit. His love never quits. If you are still crying out to Him, His strength is still there for you. He is listening and working. If you will let Him, He will fuel you in this fight. It's time to get free from the bondage and get free to love and be loved.

God is fighting for you and through you. As Genesis 1 says, God gave us dominion. He has ordained that we would be masters, and with Him we shall be masters in this fight. New strength and power are available in Him.

The words on these pages are our way of joining you in the fight. Your reinforcements are here, ready to arm you with knowledge and wisdom. Let's roll.

QUESTIONS FOR REFLECTION OR DISCUSSION

1. When did you first learn about sex? Who told you? Did your parents ever talk to you?

2. What did you learn about sexuality at church; at school?

3. When did you first see pornography?

4. How many sexual stimuli do you think you ran into today? How did you respond?

2

CASUALTIES OF WAR

War is an ugly thing, but not the ugliest of things....
The person who has nothing for which he is
willing to fight, nothing which is more important
than his own personal safety...is a miserable
creature and has no chance of being free.
—JOHN STUART MILL

The man trudging through the hot, dry, East-African terrain stopped to lift his sunglasses and wipe away the sweat stinging his eyes. Standing there, he surveyed the parched landscape stretching before him then unscrewed the top on his canteen and took in a long hard gulp. After securing the top, he put the canteen away, adjusted his hat, and continued forward, moving cautiously. One always moved cautiously in Sudan. Even so, the man was ill prepared for what awaited him just beyond the next bush.

A vicious Sudanese lion poised to pounce? A cunning spotted leopard? Perhaps it was a black mamba, the most feared and dangerous snake in all of Africa, coiled to strike? Surely Sam Childers would have been equipped for any of the above. What he wasn't prepared for was what he did see: a native child—a very young child—five maybe six—male. DEAD. Legs gone, his entire lower body ripped from the torso, entrails hanging out—

Decay.

Maggots.

Flies.

Stench.

At first glance one would assume that the child had been devoured by a wild beast, but Sam knew better. He had seen the signs before. This was done by beasts all right, the most dangerous beast of all—terrorists.

For several decades civil war has been raging in Sudan. Regardless of who's to blame, it's been one of the bloodiest conflicts ever, with the highest civilian death toll of any war since World War II. Two million civilians have been massacred and four million displaced only to die slowly from starvation due to war-induced famine. The terrorists will stop at nothing to gain control. They are ruthless. They are brutal. They are pure evil. The young boy had been blown to bits by a landmine. Terrorists had planted thousands of them around villages. One minute the children would be playing soccer and the next there would be an explosion that obliterated a precious life.

It's always the children, the sons and the daughters, the women, the wives; the families pay the highest price in war. Often, the terrorists raid the villages, killing the adult males before they set fire to the huts. They rape the women, then disfigure them by cutting off their lips, ears, and breasts with machetes. The children are made to watch. Frequently they force the boys to kill their own parents and sisters. The terrorists take the boys and brainwash them. Over time, after witnessing so much killing, the boys become monsters themselves, repeating the same atrocities as their captors. It's hideous, repulsive, wicked.

Sons.

Daughters.

Mothers.

Fathers.

Husbands.

Wives.

We watch the television in disbelief. Once the reality sets in, fear grips us. We are filled with a righteous anger, and some of us cry. Because war is horrible. It's cruel. There *is* an enemy out there who wants to kill us. After all, who did the terrorists get this from? Satan is the ultimate terrorist. We can cover our eyes and pretend it isn't real. We can try not to think about it. But it *is* real. Just ask the families of the victims.

An American, Sam Childers, was in East Africa volunteering his services as a construction worker when he walked up on the decaying corpse that was once a living child. Sam knew he could not just cover his eyes. He had to do something about the atrocities he was seeing. But what can *one* man do?

ONE MAN CAN DO A LOT

After sensing God's direction, Sam Childers picked up a machine gun and began to fight for the children, risking his live to rescue them. Soon, other men joined him in the fight, forming their own little army. Now the enemy fears them. In the past decade they've saved the lives of thousands of kids and have built several orphanages. Like military compounds, the orphanages keep the enemy out, giving the kids a chance at life. The terrorists are consistently trying to kill Sam, yet time and time again, God has supernaturally protected him. The enemy has also spread various lies to try to discredit him, but Sam just keeps fighting for the kids. President Salva Kiir Mayardit of South Sudan said "The reverend Sam Childers has been a very close friend to the government for many years and is a trusted friend." President Yoweri Museveni of Uganda said, "Sam Childers is a long time devoted friend to our government and his courageous work is supported by us." In 2013, Sam was the recipient of the Mother Theresa Humanitarian Award. Other recipients of this award include the Dalai Lama.[2]

There's another amazing thing about Sam Childers. He'd be the first to tell you that he's a man with a checkered past and many flaws. Once a barroom brawler, drug addict and sex addict, Christ came in and changed his life. However, it wasn't until he began to fight for something bigger than himself that he really began to live life to the fullest. Willing to fight and even die in the process, he found real life.

One man can do a whole lot, if he is fighting for the right thing.

Here are the questions to ask yourself:

- What are you willing to fight for?

- What are you willing to die for?

- Would you fight if people were dying around you?

- Would you fight if your wife or children were being hurt or destroyed?

- Would you fight if something were destroying you? Your spiritual life? Your integrity?

There's another war raging, a civil war of sorts. It's been going on since Creation. Sadly, this war is just as horrific, just as devastating as the hideousness and pain of physical wars and terrorism with innocent casualties. There's a war going on for the *hearts* and *souls* of men. It's reached epic levels and is threatening the very fabric of generations—grandfathers, dads, sons and grandsons. You can cover your eyes and pretend it's not happening, and in most churches this is exactly what is going on. Church leaders appear to be occupied elsewhere. Perhaps they don't know how to lead the fight in this war, but their foot soldiers are getting slaughtered. Landmines planted strategically by the enemy are knocking out our men, *especially our young men*, marring their souls, changing their futures,

---

2 Sam Childers, *Another Man's War: The True Story of One Man's Battle to Save Children in the Sudan* (Nashville: Thomas Nelson, 2009).

wrecking their relationships, jeopardizing their marriages, and taking their sons and daughters captive!

We are talking about an all-out assault on the power and beauty of sex as God designed it.

We are talking about the battle with lust and pornography, sexual brokenness, sexual strongholds, and yes, even sexual addictions.

SEXOLOGY 101

The Bible is clear, crystal clear, that *sex* is good. It's a natural desire and an appetite from God, a shadow of the intimacy we will one day experience fully with Him. The amazing and wonderful intimacy between a man and his wife was purposed by our loving Creator who knew that it was not good for man to be alone. It *is* good for a man to be aroused with the beauty of his wife and to enjoy her completely.

But God had more in mind than just the act of intercourse. To speak of our *sexuality* is to speak about our identities, our images of masculinity and femininity, our attitudes and values, as well as our honor and respect for one another. Our sexuality, though influenced by our families and culture, should be defined and managed by our faith and belief in what God has spoken.

The Bible says that our bodies are members of Christ, and yet they also are a gift to one another. So as we belong to one another as husband and wife, so also we belong to Christ. (See First Corinthians 6:15, 17; 7:1-5.) In joining together in marriage, a husband and a wife are creating a new identity together. This union is so valuable to God, that we must not hurt one another, use one another, nor neglect one another. (See First Corinthians 7:5; also see First Thessalonians 4:4-7.) The Song of Solomon persuades us to let our relationship be filled with kindness and praise, with protection and character, with playfulness and laughter. The Song is the fullness of the expression in Proverbs 5:18, to "rejoice in the wife of your youth." We must guard our sex and our sexuality. We must be careful how we express our sexuality outside our marriage, lest we defile the act of marriage.

This is our challenge, for sexuality is a God-ordained dimension to our humanness. There should be no shame simply because you notice a beautiful woman. But sex is meant to be enjoyed in its purposed context. It's a beautiful way of expressing the deepest level of intimacy between man and woman. It's a gift from God, a reward to couples for taking the time to develop the social and spiritual dimensions to intimacy. We are hardwired for both sex and intimacy, so even testosterone was part of God's plan. Being a male, sexual creature made in the image of God, can be an exhilarating experience when we are enjoying sex according to His design.

But lust and sexual sin have also been a battle since perfect harmony in relationships was disrupted in the Fall. You can trace it back to the book of Genesis, where, in fact, we can read about several different sexual sins, including adultery, prostitution and incest, forms of sexual sin that people in the church are secretly acquainted with. Satan saw the beauty when Adam and Eve came together sexually, to express the intimacy of their Garden of Eden ecstasy, and he knew he had to destroy the beauty of this oneness. His games are corruption and destruction. He steals, then distorts, and we see the devastating effects of this on a regular basis, as men come into our counseling offices, broken and in deep despair. We are meeting with men who have lost everything, or they are on the verge of losing jobs, marriages and reputations, because of the inability to stop their broken, illicit sexual behavior. The sexualization of our culture, through television, grocery store magazines, endless porn sites, websites for adultery, as well as the sexual chaos of today's generations, are the enemy's missiles and landmines that assault us.

SUPERCHARGED

The reason for this deluge in brokenness and despair is that modern-day sexual exposure has burst through a ceiling. This war has been escalated to a whole new level in just the past 15 to 20 years. This is the result of the Internet. The World Wide Web can be exactly that: a web. Internet pornography is so accessible that it has snared men in a web of lust and deceit, and it is consuming and slaughtering men and boys everywhere. Once someone is hooked, they can easily get free pornography virtually anywhere—34 percent of Internet users have seen porn unintentionally![3] It's coming like a tidal wave with a level of intensity that we've never experienced before. What we're facing as a culture is insane—levels of sexual saturation that is producing compulsions and addictions with a bondage equal to that of cocaine or heroin.

It's time to wake up to this reality and do battle! This problem is rampant, storming us like an invading guerilla army and leaving in its wake devastation like that in the Sudan. Just as conventional war changed in the 21st century into a new kind of war against terrorism, what has happened because of the Internet has amped up the battle for sexual purity:

- Count to one. In that second—and every other second—almost 30,000 people are viewing pornography.

- Also happening every second—$3,075.64 is being spent on pornography.[4]

- What factor can increase the rate of infidelity by *300%?* The factor is *the regular viewing of pornography.*

- In 56% of all divorce cases, one party had an obsessive interest in porn.[5] [6]

---

3 From Covenant Eyes: Porn Stats (http://www.covenanteyes.com/2010/06/16/porn-stats-most -popular-day-to-watch-porn-is-sunday/)(Accessed February 5, 2015).

4 Jerry Ropelato, "Internet Pornography Statistics" (http://www.ministryoftruth.me.uk/wp -content/uploads/2014/03/IFR2013.pdf)(Accessed February 5, 2015).

5 From Josh McDowell, "Just1ClickAway" (http://www.just1clickaway.org/)(Accessed February 5, 2015).

6 J. Manning, Senate Testimony 2004, referencing: Dedmon, J., "Is the Internet bad for your marriage? Online affairs, pornographic sites playing greater role in divorces," 2002, press release from The Dilenschneider Group, Inc.

- 93% of boys are exposed to Internet pornography before the age of 18.[7]

Scientists and relationship experts worldwide—both Christian and secular—are acknowledging the harmful impact of pornography on men, women, and relationships. Researchers at the University of Chicago have come out declaring that pornography is dehumanizing to women. In defining porn as the sexual subordination of women, these scholars call for a ban on its pervasiveness in our culture. Their conclusion is the same as what the church has been saying for years: Pornography turns women into commodities, into mere sexual objects. These researchers close with this statement: "Women in pornographic movies are often raped and forced to act in degrading ways. But viewers of these films come to believe that these women enjoy these acts, leading men into believing that this is the way that all women like to be treated."[8] It is easy to forget the editing, directing, and payments that were used to make this lie appear to be real on screen.

Men are finding their sexual desires changed by what they see in pornography. A 2014 survey conducted by researchers at the University of Arkansas found that the more young men watched porn, the more likely they were to ask their partner to do things they had seen. The concern? Pornography is high on degrading acts and typically neglects tenderness.[9] Eighty-eight percent of pornography shows physical aggression.[10]

These statistics and research should sober every man. Sex is being destroyed by pornography. People who watch pornography have less

---

7 From Covenant Eyes: Teens and Porn: 10 Statistics you Need to Know (http://www
.covenanteyes.com/2010/08/19/teens-and-porn-10-stats-your-need-to-know/)(Accessed February
5, 2015).

8 See "Should Pornography be banned as a threat to women?" quoting Catherine A. MacKinnon
and Andrea Dworkin (http://www.csun.edu/~psy453/porno_y.htm)(Accessed December 26,
2014).

9 The Health Site December 14, 2014, "Men, Watching Porn Can Hamper Your Sexual
Performance" (http://www.thehealthsite.com/news/men-watching-porn-can-hamper-your-sexual
-performance/)(Accessed February 5, 2015).

10 From Covenant Eyes: An Ex-Porn Star Tells the Truth (http://www.covenanteyes
.com/2008/10/29/ex-porn-star-tells-the-truth-part-2/)(Accessed February 5, 2015).

sex—and the sex they have is less satisfying![11] Sex becomes an act, an exercise, anything but loving and intimate. As a result, many men don't even know how to participate in emotional closeness and non-sexual touch.

Not long ago, I (Tim) was arriving at a hotel in Atlanta, having flown in late at night, around 2:00 A.M. It was windy outside, gusting, as I approach the entrance. Suddenly the door swung open and I was standing face to face with a local call girl. At 2:00 A.M. she was just on her way out of the hotel. Merely make a passing comment, I said, "It's windy outside," and she quipped back, "Hey Baby, you're not in Kansas anymore." When it comes to the easily accessible temptations surrounding us each day—she's right! And the Wizard of Oz has no magic spell to send us back to a simpler time. We must learn to fight in the now.

Howard came in for counseling, exhausted by an Internet pornography problem that was killing his spiritual life. You wouldn't believe how it started. He had grown up in the 1960s and 70s without a pornography problem. He received Christ into his life sometime in his late twenties, married a Christian woman, had three children, and attended an excellent Bible-teaching church. He was well respected for his leadership in business and the church. But when his children were preteens, Howard bought a new computer for the children's schoolwork. Everyone had gone to bed by the time he had everything set up, including the Internet service. To ensure that Internet service was working adequately he checked out a sports website. Then he checked the news on a popular site. Before he turned off the computer, Howard remembered that other men had told him how easy it was for children to click on pornography. He didn't want that to happen to his kids, so he wondered how easy. He decided to see for himself. In only a few moments, Howard had stopped breathing. His eyes were dilated large. His pulse was racing. Howard was captivated by the images. It took only a few moments, but a Christian man with no previous problem with porn suddenly had one. And it began to grow. We

---

11 Pamela Paul, "From Pornography to Porno to Porn: How Porn Became the Norm," In
James R. Stoner and Donna Hughes (eds.), *The Social Costs of Pornography: A Collection of Papers*
(Princeton, N.J.: Witherspoon Institute, 2010), 3–20.

are not saying that viewing porn will make you an addict. But let us make this point—it can. We will explain this biologically, emotionally, and spiritually in future chapters.

Howard's battle was the usual one. He felt exhilarated but dirty; his prayer time became confessing and pleading; he would go to church but quit speaking up; he began to hate himself (which we call *shame*). His struggle had become exhausting by the time he came in for help. Trapped almost accidentally, innocently, Howard had been caught up in the war with the power of the Internet—and all of Hell.

A SOBERING REALITY

As counselors we are hearing from churchgoing families that Internet pornography is the number one problem in their homes. One poll indicated that 47 percent of families find that pornography is a problem in their home.[12] It's like a cancer destroying the family. People everywhere are "connected," but few are experiencing intimacy. Young men raised with cell phones with privacy-invading apps have been cheated into accepting relationships that are short and shallow, just like their social media messages. Eighty-seven percent of teenagers have Internet access,[13] and yet increased Internet usage is correlated with loneliness, not with connection.[14] Seventy-nine percent of youths' unwanted exposure to pornography occurs in the home.[15]

There has also been a recent explosion of what we now call "mommy porn," literature that is luring both married and single women, and even

---

12 Focus on the Family poll, October 1, 2003.

13 Pew/Internet & American Life Project, "Teens and Technology," Amanda Lenhart, July 25, 2005 (http://www.pewinternet.org/files/old-media/Files/Reports/2005/PIP_Teens_Tech _July2005web.pdf.pdf)(Accessed February 5, 2015).

14 Archibald Hart and Sylvia Hart Frejd, *The Digital Invasion* (Grand Rapids, MI: Baker, 2009).

15 Janis Wolak, Kimberly Mitchell, and David Finkelhor, "Online Victimization of Youth: Five Years Later," University of New Hampshire Crimes Against Children Research Center, 2006 (http://www.unh.edu/ccrc/pdf/CV138.pdf)(Accessed February 5, 2015).

teenage girls, into a world of inappropriate sexual fantasy.[16] Desperate to love and be loved in a broken world, it is creating for them the same damaging, unrealistic sexual expectations that pornography creates in the minds of men.

Parents or spouses can set Internet filters or check the Internet history and feel a false sense of security and relief. However, it is easy for pornography usage to be hidden in a cell phone. Half of the 38 million people who use "Pornhub" are viewing through their mobile devices.[17]

Our daughters are at great risk, because the boys they are dating and the young men they will marry are the very ones being damaged and ensnared today. Our sons and daughters are facing a myriad of temptations not available to previous generations. Seventy-one percent of teenagers admit to hiding online behavior from their parents. Thirty percent of 17-year-olds have sent a "sext" (a text message with a sexual description or picture).[18] Our teenagers are less capable of true connection and intimacy because of their online behavior—including pornography usage! And, as sociologist Dr. Jill Manning has pointed out, "Even more disturbing is the fact that the first Internet generations have not reached full maturity, so the upper limits of this impact have yet to be realized."[19]

Many men believe the lie that their lust and pornography usage only impacts them. We will expose the dangers and fallacy of that lie

---

16   While some men might get excited over the notion that their wives are interested in this type of erotica, as a society we need to press the pause button and consider the long-term repercussions. According to Shannon Ethridge, author of *The Fantasy Fallacy* (Thomas Nelson 2012), such material often causes women to project many unrealistic sexual expectations onto their husbands, just as the images in pornography lead men to expect far more from their wives than is humanly possible. Such projections are poison to an otherwise healthy marriage, and many breakups are now being dubbed "*Fifty Shades of Grey* divorces" due to these unmet expectations.

17   "Forbidden Fruit: Apple Users Consume More Porn on Mobile," TimesLIVE, June 5, 2014 (http://www.timeslive.co.za/scitech/2014/06/05/forbidden-fruit---apple-users-consume-more -porn-on-mobile)(Accessed February 5, 2015).

18   From Covenant Eyes: Sexting Statistics: What Do the Surveys Say? (http://www.covenanteyes .com/2012/01/10/sexting-statistics-what-do-the-surveys-say/)(Accessed February 5, 2015).

19   Article I. Testimony before the Subcommittee on the Constitution, Civil Rights and Property Rights Committee on Judiciary United States Senate, November 9, 2005.

throughout this book. Families, churches, and friendships are impacted. Children are impacted. Read this anonymous open letter from a woman who found pornography on her father's computer:

Dear Dad,

I want to let you know first of all that I love you and forgive you for what this has done in my life. I also wanted to let you know exactly what your porn use has done to my life. You may think that this effects only you, or even your and mom's relationships. But it has had a profound impact on me and all of my siblings as well.

I found your porn on the computer somewhere around the age of 12 or so, just when I was starting to become a young woman. First of all, it seemed very hypocritical to me that you were trying to teach me the value of what to let into my mind in terms of movies, yet here you were entertaining your mind with this junk on a regular basis. Your talks to me about being careful with what I watched meant virtually nothing.

Because of pornography, I was aware that mom was not the only woman you were looking at. I became acutely aware of your wandering eye when we were out and about. This taught me that all men have a wandering eye and can't be trusted. I learned to distrust and even dislike men for the way they perceived women in this way.

As far as modesty goes, you tried to talk with me about how my dress affects those around me and how I should value myself for what I am on the inside. Your actions however told me that I would only ever truly be beautiful and accepted if I looked like the women on magazine covers or in porn. Your talks with me meant nothing and in fact, just made me angry.

As I grew older, I only had this message reinforced by the culture we live in. That beauty is something that can only be achieved if you look like "them." I also learned to trust you less and less as what you told me didn't line up with what you did. I wondered more and more if I would ever find a man who would accept me and love me for me and not just a pretty face.

When I had friends over, I wondered how you perceived them. Did you see them as my friends, or did you see them as a pretty face in one of your fantasies? No girl should ever have to wonder that about the man who is supposed to be protecting her and other women in her life.

I did meet a man. One of the first things I asked him about was his struggle with pornography. I'm thankful to God that it is something that hasn't had a grip on his life. We still have had struggles because of the deep-rooted distrust in my heart for men. Yes, your porn watching has affected my relationship with my husband years later.

If I could tell you one thing, it would be this: Porn didn't just affect your life; it affected everyone around you in ways I don't think you can ever realize. It still affects me to this day as I realize the hold that it has on our society. I dread the day when I have to talk with my sweet little boy about pornography and its far-reaching greedy hands. When I tell him about how pornography, like most sins, affects far more than just us.

Like, I said, I have forgiven you. I am so thankful for the work that God has done in my life in this area. It is an area that I still struggle with from time to time, but I am thankful for God's grace and also my husband's. I do pray that you are past this and that the many men who struggle with this will have their eyes opened.

Love, Your Daughter

Maybe until this point you have been thinking of your own experience in this battle. But as we expand our thoughts to our family, friends, and churches, we reach the sobering realization that the war is all around us and we are not the only ones we need to fight for.

> **STRATEGY**
> Use a picture of your wife or family as the background image on your cell phone. Use it as a reminder of who you are fighting the battle for.

PURSUE, OVERTAKE, RESCUE

Awake, O sleeper, and arise from the dead, and Christ will shine on you (Ephesians 5:14 ESV).

Remember the Lord, who is great and awesome, and fight for your brothers, your sons, your daughters, your wives, and your homes (Nehemiah 4:14 ESV).

In First Samuel 30, we read the account of David and his mighty men, who have returned to their home in Ziklag, a village on the western land of the Philistines. On arriving in their village, they found the city empty! It had been burned and destroyed, and all of their wives and sons and daughters had been kidnapped and taken away by the Amalekites! The men, Scripture says, began to lose their minds. They grieved in the anguish that their families were dead. David prayed to Yahweh, perhaps wondering if it was too late, "Shall I pursue the Amalekites. Shall I overtake them?"

Yahweh answered and told him, "Pursue. Overtake. Rescue!"

David and his men pursued the Amalekites and found them in a drunken celebration, unprepared for an attack. It was twilight when David's army struck, and his band of brothers killed every marauding soldier of the Amalekite army that they confronted, striking them down one after another, until evening on the next day. David and all his men rescued their own wives, their young sons and daughters, and all the spoils of their homes that had been taken. They rescued everyone, and brought them back home.

This is our calling, men. This is war! We must rescue our wives, our sons, our daughters, our homes. We rescue them by fighting for our freedom in Christ.

We must fight for one another and for our families. Church pastors, elders and deacons, men's and women's ministry leaders, we are pleading with you. There is an elephant sitting in the pew of the church that everyone knows is there, yet nobody wants to talk about. We believe that in the next decade the greatest challenge facing the church will most certainly be dealing with the issues of sexual brokenness and shame. Period. No other issue will compete with this. If we don't show men how serious this is, and more importantly *how to be faithful and strategic in this battle*, then a passivity and hopelessness could hit our churches that would leave men all over the world spiritually broken and powerless.

Where there is no purity, there is no power.

SEXUAL HEALING

We've got to get beyond the idea that an Internet filter will fix everything. A filter only fixes the computer. The filter doesn't fix you! We've got to stop kidding ourselves into thinking we are solving the problem when we talk about external rules of accountability, like "don't join a health club with women; don't look at magazine racks; never get on an elevator alone with a strange woman."

What? Good grief. These external rules are like orange cones placed five feet into the trees, meant to keep us from veering off the road. These external rules can help but cannot heal or transform the internal heart of a man. When you want what you want, and your mind is consumed, you will plow through your self-imposed barriers and send orange cones flying in all directions, just to taste the forbidden fruit! We must get more serious and stop playing games.

James grew up in a conservative Christian home, involved in his local church. He went off to the state university to play football. One night some of the boys on the football team came to the athlete's dorm with a pornographic video. James didn't want to be the only one to bail out, so he stayed and watched. One look at pornography and it had the same effect as crack cocaine. He was hooked. That one night opened the door to years and years of a porn obsession. It awakened a roaring lion that devoured him.

The double life that James began to live seemed to work at first. Since he had responded to the call to ministry earlier in life, all of James' energy was ultimately reduced to the balancing of these two lives: the devotion to Bible study and ministry skills, and an obsession with the secret life of pornography and masturbation. It was a stress-filled life. Pornography robbed James of his heart, his creative ability, and ultimately the hope of his faith in Christ. After years of failure and discouragement, defeated in every attempt to stop, James came to hate what his life had become. One night! One pornographic video! Now he was a textbook case study of the power of porn to destroy a young man's life.

Now, some of you may be reading this, rolling your eyes and thinking, "Man, are you guys overreacting! Sure I may struggle a little with lust, but I'm basically a good guy; I try to honor the women I date." Or, "I love my wife and kids; I join them in church; I'm not having an affair." If that's what you're thinking, then consider where you stand in light of these recent statistics below, from interviews with Christian men about their porn usage.[20]

- 97% of Christian men acknowledge that they have looked at porn.

- 80% of Christian men do not have any Internet filters or blocks on their computer.

- 65% of Christian men viewed porn at work, hiding it from their wives.

- 25% of Christian men admit to erasing Internet history to conceal their browsing.

- 64% of Christian men view porn at least once a month.

---

20 Proven Men Ministries, with the Barna Group, 2014 survey (http://www.provenmen .org/2014pornsurvey).

- 55% of married Christian men view porn at least once a month.

- 37% of Christian men look at porn several times a week.

- 77% of those ages 18–30 view porn at least once a month.

- 32% of Christian men ages 18–30 think they are addicted to porn. (Another 12% are not sure.)

Every sexual addict we counsel never intended to be an addict. They tell us that they never thought they would go as far as they did. But it's easy to get lost in this world. You might not be an addict, but that's according to your own self-assessment. You may look great on the outside and have the appearance of godliness, but if you're not dealing with what's in your heart, then you are minimizing the damage being done. As counselors, we have heard many men state that finding pornography was the *worst* thing that happened to them. If a man is addicted, he is 23 times more likely to say that discovering pornography was the worst thing to ever happen to him.[21] The worst thing in his whole life! Even if you are only looking at porn a few times a year, we know that you hate it! You hate what it is doing to your heart with the fear and the shame of the secret.

- Pornography damages relationships, especially your ability to see God in your life.

- Pornographic images cloud your mind when you are making love to your wife.

- Sexual impurity is compromising your ability to discern and hear the Holy Spirit.

- Fantasy and lust are destroying your ability to dream and imagine for God.

---

21   From Josh McDowell, "Just1ClickAway" (http://www.just1clickaway.org/)(Accessed February 5, 2015).

- Sexual sin makes you passive and weak-willed, as you feel too ashamed to guard your own heart and your family against the spiritual attacks.

When we understand the above, First Corinthians 6:9-11 has a deeper meaning:

> *Or do you not know that the unrighteous will not inherit the kingdom of God? Do not be deceived; neither fornicators, nor idolaters, nor adulterers, nor effeminate, nor homosexuals, nor thieves, nor the covetous, nor drunkards, nor revilers, nor swindlers, will inherit the kingdom of God. Such were some of you; but you were washed, but you were sanctified, but you were justified in the name of the Lord Jesus Christ and in the Spirit of our God* (ESV).

Not dealing with the internal issues in your heart is like juggling unpinned grenades. Sin, especially sexual sin, will take you places you never thought you would go. It can drive you to the depths of despair, cause you heartache, and ruin your life. We've seen the scenario unfold over and over again with men like Howard and James.

So many have lost hope and quit trying to break free. They have reached the "what-does-it-matter" phase and have become numb, so defeated by their sexual sin, with no hope of ever gaining control, that they give up and say, "what's the use; what does it matter; church doesn't work; God doesn't work; nothing will work."

We get that—but that doesn't have to be your story.

If you are reading this book, chances are the enemy is trying to take you down. Perhaps you've lost hope. Regardless of how much you have failed and are despairing, don't give up. There is hope! Freedom can be a reality! We see it every day!

What can one man do?

If you are still crying out for God to help, the seeds of hope are still in you. If one can get free, then others will have hope. Marriages can be restored and strengthened. If one young man can find the way to freedom, he can help his friends get free, and change the tone of their campus ministry group. If a handful of married men in the church can get free, they can alter the spiritual culture of their Men's Ministry, and radically transform their church.

Isn't it time?

One man can do a whole lot.

QUESTIONS FOR REFLECTION OR DISCUSSION

1. Have a conversation about the different statistics listed in this chapter. How many of these statistics are surprising? Which of the statistics are alarming?

2. Have a conversation about how serious you think your church is in dealing with this issue? Does your church have a Men's Ministry that takes this seriously? What would you like to see your Men's Ministry do about this?

3. Discuss your thoughts on the power of pornography to hinder your ability to "see" God in your life.

3

SEX ON THE BRAIN

*Postcoitum omnis animal triste. ("After
sex every creature is sad.")*
—ANCIENT ROMAN PROVERB

Your greatest sex organ is your brain. In fact, if you didn't have a brain, sex wouldn't be much fun at all. What makes something thrilling and exciting is the way we *think* and *feel* about it. Thinking and feeling, and the resulting behaviors, are the essential functions of the brain.

The brain can either be our ally or our enemy in the fight of our lives. Most of us get the impression that our brain is definitely our enemy in the realm of the sexual battle, simply because of the images and memories stored there. But if we can understand what is happening with our brains, that awareness can increase our power and ability to overcome the defeat and discouragement of sexual challenges.

Two things are happening across our brain at all times. One of these things is electrical, and the other is chemical. The electrical represents our thoughts. The chemicals represent our emotions. Our thoughts are shooting across the brain all the time, and in their wake flow the chemicals, created by glands inside the brain. If you have a pleasurable experience in life, then your glands will produce positive, "feel-good" chemicals. If you have a painful experience in life, then your glands will produce negative, "downer" chemicals. The brain, essentially, is its own community with its own electrical power plant and pharmacies. The brain has a Data Collection Department, Interpretation & Meanings Department, a Linguistic Department, a Pleasure Center, a Memorial Library, an Action Center, as well as a Toxic Waste Center, all linked together with an intricate electro-chemical highway system.

Our lives are filled with pleasurable experiences, painful experiences, and mundane experiences. Information is received, perceived, and stored with every experience we have. You know that, but here's something you maybe didn't know: In response to that information, as the chemicals are secreted throughout the body, some of these chemicals contain molecules with an electromagnetic charge. These molecules often *carry a photocopy of our experiences that have been sorted and filed in the mind.*

Oh, no.

Oh, yes. Can you see where we might have a problem with our sexual struggles? Those pornographic images are being stored and filed somewhere in the brain, much like a temporary Internet file that cannot be deleted.

Let's illustrate what is happening with lust and pornography, by using two other familiar illustrations. When you were a child, you might have had your favorite snack food down at the corner food mart. Any chance you had to get that snack, you were going to get it. Today, as an adult, when you are under stress or conflict, and you need relief or comfort, you can simply drive past a similar food mart, and at that moment think of that favorite snack (an apple fritter or a donut) and say, "I'd love to have that!" Just the thought of that sweet taste can start to produce the same effect in your brain.

Now, let's take a look at what sexual thoughts, both good and bad, do to our brains by comparing them to alcohol. It is likely that you know someone who is consumed each weekend with the goal of having a little alcohol for the purpose of creating a slight "buzz." The goal is not all-out drunkenness, but only to create a desired altered state. The "buzz" is created by drinking the chemicals in the alcoholic beverage, which then influence your brain. Your "buzz" is created by chemicals you already have in your brain, by overwhelming them with more chemicals from the beverage. When you ingest the alcoholic drink, you have "hijacked" your brain, creating that altered state. Here's the point: *Entertaining lustful thoughts and viewing pornography does the same thing to your brain!*

It can cause a chemical cocktail to be stirred up in the glands of the brain, and your brain can get hijacked by these chemicals. In fact, those chemicals will be produced even when you simply remember an actual sexual experience, a lustful fantasy, or a sexual image you saw. Your brain is subject to being influenced by the chemical cocktail, and the behavior is not far behind.

Every bottle of alcohol is made to certain standards back at the distillery, so that every bottle has the same power to create the desired effect. Every bottle works the same. Alcohol is consistent, and while serious addicts may realize that the amount needed to create the desired impact will increase, the type of impact that alcohol has stays the same. Every bottle will influence your brain. Additionally, consider a casino. Everything from room temperature, the color of the walls, placement of seating, and background music is carefully selected to encourage specific (risk-taking) behaviors. So it is with pornography. The multi-billion dollar pornography industry and Hollywood are just as purposeful as the distillery in creating an experience that has a specific impact. Sexually explicit images can hijack your brain!

You must understand what can happen with every sexual experience and every pornographic image (whether from the Internet or fantasy) as it is stored, collated, sorted, and photocopied on to these particular molecules with a magnetic charge. These are being sent throughout your body affecting and influencing such things as your heart rate, your breathing rate, your stress, your anxiety level, your despair and your shame. When you add continued behavior, it even further solidifies the pattern. Acting on the images and urges is like taking a document to the notary to make it official!

You may have seasons where lustful images are not a part of your daily thoughts. But unless you know how to fix what's going on, suddenly you will glance at a billboard, or see a woman across the room, or simply have a flashback to an old image, and you will find yourself falling right back into the old ruts. Suddenly, your brain starts a flurry of activity that will leave you spinning all over again. Chemicals in your brain can create an emotional state that can last for hours, even days, wrecking your disposition, sending you into thoughts and a flood of emotions that will affect your work, your relationships, and your spiritual life.

Don't despair at this. Once we have explained what is happening, we will show you the way out.

BRAIN FUNCTION: A PRIMER

The chemistry of the human brain is highly complex and we will not be able to shed much on that complexity in this book. The good news, however, is twofold:

First, much of the general function of the brain can be readily understood by most people.

Second, there is more and more research being done in how the brain functions and how addictions develop.

Therefore, let the material offered here be a primer of sorts.

The brain has three main sections; hindbrain, midbrain, and forebrain. The forebrain includes the cortex/neocortex (cognitive center—rationality, ideas) and interacts with the limbic system (affect—feelings). The feeling of pleasure is produced and regulated by a circuit of specialized nerve cells within the limbic system.

Nearly 100 billion neurons (nerve cells) are present in the brain— and a strongly stimulated neuron can fire a thousand times a second.

Sensory information is processed *chemically* in the brain. A person does not "think" or "feel" in a vacuum. Real chemicals are involved.

Incoming data may be filtered through "concepts"—words that have become clustered together in a form of chemical shorthand for more rapid processing. Or, the data may go directly into visual, aural, and other forms of chemical coding.

The chemical "factories" in the brain are the neurons. The chemicals that do this coding are called neurotransmitters—22 of them have been identified up to the present time. More may exist. The neurons are actually hormone factories—they release chemicals such as dopamine, serotonin, endorphins, and so forth. These chemicals assign the incoming sensory data in two ways—the sensory data is assigned to a storage area in the brain, such as the Memory Center, or perhaps the Pleasure Center. This makes retrieval of the data possible.

The chemicals generated by neurons send on sensory data to other hormone-producing centers in the body. In the case of sexual sensory data, the areas that produce adrenaline and sex hormones (such as testosterone) are triggered.

And all of this occurs in split-second timing—faster than a person can sound out the ten syllables in "psycho-neurological pathway."

We should note that incoming sensory data is coded according to *what* has been perceived, and according to the degree of *intensity* of the data.

CHART OF NEUROTRANSMITTERS AND THEIR FUNCTION	
Neurotransmitter	Primary Function
Serotonin	Regulates mood; increases self-confidence; creates a feeling of safety and security; can increase sleepiness and appetite.
Dopamine	Regulates mood, cognition, sleep, attention and memory; influences motivation and the punishment/reward system.
Norephinephrine	Impacts the fight/flight syndrome, acts as both a stress hormone and as a neurotransmitter; impacts heart rate and glucose levels; impacts attention and focus; also called noradrenaline.
Acetylcholine	Activates muscles (contraction); influences memory and cognition; it is the primary neurotransmitter within the autonomic nervous system; regulates brain processing speed.
Gamma-aminobutyric Acid (GABA)	Reduces excessive brain activity; reduces the impact of stress and irritability; promotes a state of calm; helps in relaxation and reduces anxiety.
Epinephrine	Initiates the flight/fight syndrome; acts as both a stress hormone and a neurotransmitter; promotes secondary release of endorphins; also called adrenaline.
Endorphin	Prevents nerve cells from releasing more pain signals increases feelings of well-being.

Let's break these chemicals down.

The first chemical, adrenaline (or epinephrine), which we know and refer to mostly by its effect, is produced by the adrenal glands on top of our kidneys. Adrenaline gives us a "high" and causes us to feel motivated and energized. Dopamine follows with a rush of pleasurable feeling.

There are many activities that can kick-start adrenaline production: driving by the store and thinking of those donuts, getting energized by an intense workout, completing a work assignment with a looming deadline, hopping on a Jet Ski or a motorcycle, parachuting from the edge of a cliff, getting your first kiss from your new girlfriend in junior high school, taking the field for the opening kickoff, or even putting big money down on 17-Red at the roulette table. Anything that creates and sustains fear, anxiety, panic, or risky excitement can cause adrenaline to be produced and stimulated. Oh, yes, and *sex* produces adrenaline and dopamine.

Think about the activities and environments you pursue. Are your weekends geared for the sake of stirring up your adrenaline? Adrenaline and dopamine, again, are chemicals. They are part of a cluster of certain chemicals that also gives us what we call the "happy" brain. Happy brain chemicals are those that are flowing when we fall in love, when we accomplish a big goal, when we ace a test, when we "nail" an interview and get hired, or when we bungee-jump off a bridge. And, yes, when we visualize sexual images. These chemicals produce an intense feeling of excitement and pleasure in our bodies. When these chemicals subside in our brains, there is a letdown, and the letdown drives us to rev up the happy chemicals again. This is also associated with why men—men who love God, men who are married to wonderful wives, attractive wives, with satisfying sex lives—will still fall into a lustful thought life or infidelity. They become addicted to the happy brain, and cannot stand the letdown. The letdown feels so blue and empty that it drives them to seek out more sex, risky sex, gambling sex. The more risk involved, the better, since that will create more "happy" chemicals!

Do you see the issue? Your brain and the chemicals produced in the brain's glandular system can drive your sexual energy and pleasure. You think that you are extra lonely, that you just need a girlfriend, or that your wife doesn't "get" you, or that you are more needy than the average man. No! Your real challenge is your raging chemical state of mind!

Lust, that intense sexual desire, starts the cycle. Lust sends you to imagine or seek out sexually explicit images. Entertaining these thoughts can move one to self-sex. That cycle is so consistent in delivering the chemical reward the body and mind were seeking, that men will do it again and again. This pattern will lead to ruts in the man's life. A rut is an engrained pattern of thought or behavior that has been traveled before and is easy to default to. These ruts can come to have a strong hold. Such strongholds become the seeds of addiction. Once the adrenaline gets kick-started, it takes a man to a place where it is difficult to shut the process down.

To overcome and defeat your sexual bondage, it is very important to realize what is happening in your brain. Knowledge is power, and understanding the addiction cycle can help you jump out of it. This understanding can be a huge part of the puzzle for you, and can give you power to discern and make healthier choices.

THE SEXUAL, CHEMICAL COCKTAIL

Sex operates on a clearly defined cycle. Watch the pattern that unfolds here. The sexual response cycle consists of five stages:

Initiation. When my wife flirts with me in the grocery store, or she gives me that longing look, a trigger trips the switch of desire, and I get the notion that, if I play my cards right, we might get physical tonight. This is the beginning of initiation in my brain. It can happen in the kitchen, when your wife gives you that look or that touch. The pleasure center of your brain begins to secrete dopamine. Your eyes dilate. Your mood picks up. Your energy increases.

Excitement. As we make our way to the couch, and I see desire in my wife's eyes, I feel the adrenaline go further into my body. As you move to the bedroom, and watch your wife undress, you move to the next level of adrenaline flow. You get an adrenaline-induced excitement that is activated and felt in your body, and then starts to affect your brain with sexual arousal. The next chemical in the cluster is called dopamine. Dopamine is what makes the brain focus. It is produced as the brain subconsciously recalls the rewarding experience of past sexual relations. Dopamine increases blood flow in the body, and you know why blood flow is good. Excitement grows with the pleasure of the moment. James Brown starts singing in my mind, "I Feel Good…I knew that I would!"

Stimulation. As my wife and I begin to touch one another, a third chemical is produced, oxytocin. This is a cleansing chemical; it cleanses away the negative, "downer" chemicals in the brain. It is also the chemical that bonds your brain to the experience. That's why the sexual experience causes you to "forget" for the moment about the pain of your lives. This chemical creates a sense of well-being, even in non-sexual touching. For example, it is the "bonding" chemical that was first felt in our bodies when we nursed at our mother's breast. Meaningful touch, both sexual and nonsexual, triggers the creation of oxytocin.

Orgasm. The next chemical, norepinephrine, is well known as an anti-depressant, when this chemical spikes it triggers the ejaculation. It is also the hormone that creates a vigilant concentration, lending itself to help with the creation of memories. And your present sexual experience with this ecstasy of orgasm is a locked-in memory! That explains why we are so aware of every feeling at the moment of orgasm, as it induces a euphoria in the brain, an excitement in the body, and causes our heart to beat faster.

Relaxation. After the orgasm there is a calming effect in the brain and body, initiated by the chemicals called endorphins. Interestingly, the structure of these chemicals is very similar to heroin, and has a similar function as that illegal drug: they reduce pain, induce pleasure, and slow the heart rate.[22] With our stress reduced from this chemical cocktail our minds are suddenly free from stress. One of the reasons men don't do pillow talk after sex is that we are so relaxed that our mind suddenly is filled with fresh, inspiring ideas about football, what the real answer is to that question we missed on the quiz, how many sales calls we will make next week, just what is wrong with the lawn mower and where we can get that part to fix it, what additions we should make to the hunting camp, etc.

---

22   C. George Boeree, "Neurotransmitters," copyright 2003, 2009 (http://webspace.ship.edu/ cgboer/genpsyneurotransmitters.html) (accessed December 24, 2014).

Also, endorphins are the very chemical that animals use to hibernate. No wonder we men roll over and go to sleep so quickly—much to the dismay of our wives!

One more thing, the endorphins act as a natural painkiller for the body. Endorphins are also called "endogenous morphine." Morphine! The painkiller. Fascinating, huh? Note that there is an innate problem with the cliché of a wife denying sex because of "a headache"—sex will actually function in the body like a painkiller! If it were not for the five senses "telling" my brain what I am doing, my brain wouldn't even know the difference between having sex or entertaining lustful images. The same process is happening with either act! In fact, I could be eating an amazing dessert, snorting cocaine, or bungee jumping, and my brain wouldn't even know the difference, if it were not for the Visual Center telling me what I am looking at. As I (Mark) have written elsewhere[23] the front end of the sexual experience is having the same effect on our brain as cocaine. Oxytocin has the same effect on the brain as marijuana, and the latter part of the sexual cycle has the same effect as heroin. No wonder it is so easy to get addicted to it. No wonder we enjoy it so much. Sex is a high!

Here is why this is so important, and how we get into trouble: the Law of Diminishing Returns. What we mean by this is that the more you put into your brain, the more it will take next time to achieve the same effect. Remember, when your girlfriend took your hand the first time? Wasn't it amazing? That's all you did that first night as a 12-year-old, just hold hands, but it was heavenly.

This process is even more dangerous for teenagers. Teenagers are often exposed to porn before they are exposed to a healthy relationship. They are not only teaching their brain to get turned on by images on

---

23 Mark Laaser, *Becoming a Man of Valor* (Kansas City, MO: Beacon Hill Press, 2011), 60.

a screen—they are teaching their brain to get turned on *primarily* by images on a screen![24]

Lust and desire will always *progress*. You may have spent all week on cloud nine after holding hands with your 12-year-old girlfriend. The next weekend, however, you are not going to be satisfied with merely holding hands. Hello, next level! A hug. A kiss. An embrace. From that night on, your physical relationship will keep escalating. That's due to the law of diminishing returns. Our brains can be so stimulated that some of us will want more and more and more and more. This progression will lead to ruts. With every experience, the tolerance level will rise, requiring an escalation in order to experience the same high as the last time, for good and bad. The chemicals in our brain want more—which can mean more frequent viewing of pornography or viewing pornography that displays more illicit acts. This desire puts men in the Red Zone.

To emphasize the point:

> *You are being unhealthy or even destructive when you cope in life by purposely altering your brain's chemistry apart from intimacy with God, your wife, and your friends.*

Married men can misuse sex this way. Instead of being an expression of oneness, sex can become a "drug." We can use sex to feel better after a miserable day, using it to medicate. This is unloving and insensitive to your wife—unless your wife, knowing you had a bad day, offers to make love with you as a way to comfort you. That could be a loving gesture on her part, amazingly understanding. More often, men do not have such loving communication with their wives, and instead remain silent and brooding, ignoring the wife all evening until she gets in bed, then initiating sex selfishly as a way of creating their own escape and getting "high." This is an unhealthy sexual pattern, to use sex only to change the way they feel. It is taking, not giving.

---

24 Wilson, G. (2013), "Adolescent Brain Meets Highspeed Internet Porn" (video) (http://yourbrainonporn.com/adolescent-brain-meets-highspeed-internet-porn) (Accessed February 5, 2015).

A second problem for marriage is that if a husband is using pornography and self-sex to get "high" on his own, then he loses interest in making love to his wife. Asking her, getting turned down by her, perhaps working all day to increase intimacy with her—this is all too hard! It is much easier to look at porn and self-medicate. This creates a state in the marriage referred to as "sexual anorexia." A man can train his heart and his mind to go elsewhere, to pornography, instead of cultivating a desire for his wife's body.

Strangely, when couples use sex this way, it can lead to boredom in their sexual lives. The reason for the boredom is because their lovemaking is not loving. It is not an expression of their intimacy, but rather a way for individual escape. They are in the same bed, escaping from life's discomfort together, but not connecting with one another. They are using the other person to get "high" from the chemical cocktail of the sexual cycle. It is sex without intimacy, sex without love. It is avoiding intimacy through sex. This lack of intimacy and bonding is what makes for boredom.

The power of the chemicals in the brain should be matched by the power of spiritual intimacy. God created the power of the chemical cocktail as a way of strengthening the "high" of *intimacy*. This is why looking at porn, lusting and going to self-sex are so dangerous for men. You can be sowing the seeds of addiction by creating the ruts of lust, and self-sex can get a stronghold over you. Many young men are spending hours and hours on Internet porn. They are training themselves to return to those behaviors whenever they feel the emptiness and loneliness of painful relationships. Believing that this will all magically end at the marriage altar may be one of the biggest fantasies of all! Even in loving marriages, the feelings of emptiness and loneliness occur. And when they do, the rut of viewing pornography has been imprinted into their brains.

In marital sex, as God intended, the chemicals are what make us "addicted" and bonded to our wives. That's a good thing. It's as if God wanted us to be lost in each other's love. This makes sense when you read the proverb: "Rejoice in the wife of your youth.... Let her breasts fill you at all times with delight; be *intoxicated* always in her love" (Proverbs 5:18-19, ESV, emphasis added).

Now that you know what is going on chemically in your brain when you are delighting in your wife's breasts, it makes you wonder if God couldn't wait for the twentieth century, so He could grin at all the angels when neuroscientists discovered the chemical release He had created for the brain during sex. Our God is an awesome God, and His gift of sex is powerful. We write this book in the hopes that we will be better stewards of His gift, and that stewardship includes healthy intimacy with our wives, sharing the grace of life with them (see 1 Peter 3:7), having sex for oneness and not for our own selfish high.

This process of healthy intimacy with our wives requires that we learn how to manage and superintend our brains and the chemicals. Breaking these patterns and dealing in a healthy way with sexual triggers can also be managed better when we know that so much of the excitement is chemical.

QUESTIONS FOR REFLECTION OR DISCUSSION

1. Do you remember your first kiss? What was that like? How did the experience of kissing escalate into your desire for more? Discuss the effect of increasing tolerance.

2. Do you think you ever crave sex with your wife for the sole purpose of relieving stress or dealing with a negative emotion?

3. What do you do when your wife says "no" to sex? Do you pout, argue, plea? Or do you go downstairs and turn to lust and self-sex?

4

OUR PLASTIC BRAIN

We destroy arguments [strongholds—thoughts, purposes]
and every lofty opinion raised against the knowledge of
God, and take every thought captive to obey Christ.

—2 CORINTHIANS 10:5 ESV

Barry had wanted to remain a virgin until marriage. At a youth retreat during his junior year in high school, he had signed a card pledging himself to that end. But once he got to college, things suddenly overwhelmed him. The cute girl in his PoliSci class had found a way to introduce herself to him at the Student Center. She lived in the girl's dorm next to his. Though she said she was raised in a church, it didn't seem to have had much effect on her. On their second date, their kissing got heavy, and she took Barry's hand and rubbed it over her breasts. Barry knew that he wouldn't survive long, so he found a way to be busy the next few days and weekends, until she moved on to someone else. Barry had saved himself from losing his virginity, but his brain had tripped a switch. He had now seen. He had now touched. His hands had now gone where they had never gone before. What was worse, his *brain* had now gone where it had never gone before. Barry found himself fantasizing about this girl night after night in his dorm room. Lust and self-sex became a frequent routine, as he wrestled with the visions that danced in his head. Shame kept Barry from seeking help, making his battle both complicated and energized by its secrecy.

Derek had been caught in an affair, and his wife was devastated. As she vacillated between deep anguish and fury, their counseling sessions were painful even for their Christian counselor. As is common in situations like this, Derek still wrestled with the feelings of attraction and the emotions of connection and belonging that he had with the other woman. His mind continued to be filled with longing and memories that thrilled, haunted and tortured him, especially because the thoughts in his mind about his wife were now thoughts of distance, anger, and boredom. His brain was wired in both directions, and so he was struggling with reattaching to his wife. As they were guided through the restoration process, Derek confessed at one of his individual sessions, "I don't know how I will get this other woman out of my mind. The images of her in my head are so strong, and they trigger such a powerful desire. I'm going to go crazy!"

Barry's and Derek's minds are in a real fix. Those images and memories of physical intimacy can trigger the chemical cocktail we saw in the last chapter, sending them into orbit! Idle moments during the day when their minds run to hidden memories of her body—that's all it takes. With simply a thought, adrenaline will start flowing as the chemicals stir up their feelings. Their minds and emotions will start racing with desire. This creates a tough battle as it is; adding to the problem, Derek is seeking comfort from his wife's verbal assaults on him (understandable, as she battles with her own pain of betrayal), and Barry's loneliness also wants comfort. Such triggers help keep fresh in their minds all of their sensual, lustful memories, every last wild one.

How will they find relief?

How will they break the power of their memories?

They can actually do both, and it's because their brains are plastic.

TRANSFORMING THE MIND

Yes, Barry's and Derek's brains are plastic—and yours is too! No, not the kind of plastic that you handle in everyday consumer products. By plastic we mean it is pliable, capable of being molded or shaped. The neuroscientist today would say that there is a *neuroplasticity* to our brains. This means, our brains can change. That's good news! Barry and Derek need it.

Neuroscience, the study of the brain, has grown exponentially in the last 30 years or so. Scientists have discovered that the brain has the ability to rewire itself. The electrochemical networks of our brains are not set in stone. The brain has the ability, through a person's focused redirection, to change and compensate and grow in a different direction. Even our intelligence (IQ) is not fixed. Anyone's intelligence level can grow and develop as we learn and use new information.

Old-school psychology told us that our brains do not grow nor change much after childhood. Trauma and injury, it was believed, would leave permanent damage. Today we know this not to be true. The brain can heal. The brain can change. It can adjust to trauma, and rewire itself. Your choice of what to think about is, of course, based on your thoughts, and every person can have full control over their thoughts.

In other words, *what* you choose to think about and *how* you think about it (that is, the *mind*), especially in relationships, can cause your brain to be rewired.

Good news! "We have the mind of Christ" (1 Corinthians 2:16). No matter what years of looking at pornography have done to your brain, embracing the mind of Christ with the plasticity of your brain can change your brain and the way you think. Our brains can be reformatted, as we exchange old ways of thinking for new ones. This is what the Spirit of God is doing as we seek to be transformed by what the Apostle Paul called the renewing of our minds: "Do not conform to the pattern of this world, but be transformed by the renewing of your mind. Then you will be able to test and approve what God's will is—his good, pleasing and perfect will" (Romans 12:2). As you renew your mind, you can literally heal your brain.

In the struggle with lust, fantasy, and pornography, our brains develop a routine pattern of association. Through our eyes, the Visual Center of the brain receives a sexual image. Then, an electrochemical "picture" is taken to the Pleasure Center, where the brain's activity stimulates the glands in the brain system to produce a chemical cocktail dominated by adrenaline and dopamine. The adrenaline goes back to the Visual Center to tell the eyes to keep that exciting data coming. The dopamine goes back to the Pleasure Center to declare that "feeling good" is coming. The connection from the Visual Center to the Pleasure Center becomes a pathway, an electrochemical "trail," if you will. The more we take in the images, the more that the pathway gets worn. Every time I look lustfully at a woman or at pornographic images, I am stimulating and entrenching that pathway. Thus, scientists call it a Pleasure Pathway.

Later, without any new visual images from the Visual Center, the memory can arise on its own, up from the Memorial Library in the brain. The memory will jump on the same pathway and run over to the Pleasure Center and start knocking on the door. The Pleasure Center will remember, "Oh, yeah! She was beautiful," and send an electrical message to the Emotional Center to stir up the production of adrenaline and endorphins, and the whole process can run its course all over again. This helps us understand what is meant when a man says he feels "drawn" to the behavior.

Here's the point: As the electrical and chemical charges are racing across the brain, the brain is being wired. Neurological pathways are being created and entrenched. Lustful imaginations are being set down according to certain patterns. James 1:14 says it this way, "But each person is tempted when he is lured and enticed by his own desire" (ESV) We are looking and lusting and firing off neurons, *and neurons that fire together, wire together!*[25]

We must get this. We must see what we are doing to ourselves!

---

25   Norman Doidge, *The Brain That Changes Itself* (New York: Penguin Books, 2007), 63.

Viewing porn is not always going to create a porn sex addict—but it *can*. There is too much at risk to ignore this.

Do you see? From the time you see your first pornographic image as a boy, you can begin setting down and establishing entrenched neurological pathways in the brain and strongholds in the mind. Each time you see more porn or each time you recall old images, *you are strengthening this neurological pathway*, making it stronger and stronger until it no longer is a simple pathway. You are developing ruts in the brain that look like the dense system of the highways of the German Autobahn!

Now, let's add God to this mixture. When a man who is strong goes to church or the campus Bible study group, and the topic is sexual purity, it's natural to want to slink down in the seat. Enter *defeat* and *shame,* as the mind reviews the lustful activities during the past week. These two, defeat and shame, are also made up of thoughts/neurons/chemicals/emotions. Thus, every day that I try to read my Bible and pray, but instead of focusing on worship, I am hindered by thinking of myself as a "failure, a despicable lust-bucket," I am now laying down another new pathway in my brain, a pathway of defeat and shame!

Throw all of this in one big soup—the chemicals of lust and the chemical toxins of personal failure—and we now have a mixture primed for continual spiritual defeat and discouragement. These lust-filled neurological pathways and the shame-filled neurological pathways—both are easily triggered, and in a sense medicated—by more sensory data. The brain and the mind are both affected and involved. This is why we will often hear a man in counseling say to us, "It seems like I've always got naked women on my mind!" The reason why? He does!

But let's go back to the good news—we can *rewire* our brains and *retrain* our minds.

We can rewrite new pathways full of new electrical thoughts, thoughts of goodness and purity, along with new chemicals of love and peace. Let's show you how. First, a personal story of hope.

I (Mark) once had the privilege of participating in a study of men whose brains had been on sex for years. At the psychiatry department of a major university, the team of neuroscientists and researchers wanted to monitor our brain activity at the time that our eyes were exposed to pornography, including also the observation of sensations in other parts of the body. The brain activity was measured by FMRI, Functional Magnetic Resonance Imaging, which works by detecting the electrical activity that occurs on the top of the brain in response to the images or activities that come through the Visual Center. Wherever the brain is active, there is an increase in blood flow to that area. When the Pleasure Center is activated with sexual images, then that part of the brain will "light up" with the imaging of more intense blood and oxygen flow.

I was asked to participate because, though I had spent about 25 years looking regularly at pornography, at the time of this study I had nearly 15 years of sexual sobriety with no pornography. I, too, was very interested in how my brain would function.

When I was hooked up and wired to the FMRI scanner, the researchers then showed various clips of pornographic pictures, including a 90-second video of a couple engaged in erotic, sexual behavior. Because of my disciplined pursuit of a renewed mind and sexual healing and recovery in my life, the pornography actually made me sad and hurt (because of my past). I was not aroused in a deviant way. When the test was over, I figured that the researchers were going to tell me that there was no oxygenated blood flow to the Pleasure Center of my brain. But that was not the case.

The head of the project told me that the Pleasure Center of my brain actually lit up like a Christmas tree throughout the test! The years of pornography were still stored in the Memorial Library of my brain, but I did not feel the adrenaline, the dopamine, nor any of the rush of the chemicals related to sexual arousal. The brain's old wiring was still there, but my mind had been retrained!

Though the original pathways "lit up" during the test, the research team observed something else. My brain had actual, new pathways that had been created to override the original pathways. At the sight of pornographic images, the mental training that I had done over the previous

15 years had given me the ability to avoid sexual *arousal*. The old pathways are still there, and should I foolishly choose to return to them, I will immediately be defeated by them. But—the good news again—we can "rewire" our brains. Because of their neuroplasticity, we can use our minds to train our brains to produce healthy sexual behavior. We can train ourselves to turn away from porn, and disengage from the chemical "high" that it presently triggers in us. It begins by learning to control our minds in "taking every thought captive to obey Christ" (see 2 Corinthians 10:5).

TAKING THOUGHTS CAPTIVE TO CHRIST

We can rewire our brains by taking the most chemically charged thoughts in our minds captive to Christ.[26] Let's start with our sexual fantasies. Most of our thought life that awakens desire in us is our fantasy life. Seeing an object of attraction may get the chemicals flowing, but fantasizing will take it to a higher level. Fantasies trigger our adrenaline, they get our blood pumping and our heart beating faster. Once this trigger-cycle has started, we will be quite weak to stop it from going further. Therefore, if we can take our fantasies captive to Christ, then we can strip them of this power that leads to lust, porn, and self-sex.

To take our thoughts captive to Christ we must analyze our fantasies. If we were to do this, we would come up with a few keen insights about what drives our fantasies. Here is what we have learned as counselors, talking to hundreds, even thousands, of men who battle to control their minds.

1. Most of our sexual fantasies, if not all, reveal the story of a deeply needy and hungry soul. We are made for relationship, hardwired for intimacy with God and significant others, created to love and to be loved. But life is filled with brokenness, and often it's not the way it is supposed to be with God or others. So we are left empty and longing for more. Our souls were made to be loved, nurtured, accepted and affirmed. When we don't

---

26 Mark has written an entire book on the subject of this section, *Taking Every Thought Captive* (Kansas City, MO: Beacon Hill, 2011).

get this, our souls will still long for it. Some of our fantasies are about dreaming of a future where we get that which we long for.

Some grew up feeling inadequate and incomplete, not well-affirmed and approved of by the girls in school. Sexual fantasies can bring this fulfillment. Imaginary lovers never disappoint. To a young man, they are nurturing, worshiping, affirming, and accepting. Isn't that what fantasy and even porn promise? But it's a false intimacy!

If you have rarely been honored and respected as a man, your soul will still long for this. Analyze your fantasies to see if this is your longing. Are you dreaming of being filled, at long last, by the women of your fantasies? Your fantasy will reveal that you need healing in your heart, a healing that lust and self-sex are robbing from you.

> ## STRATEGY
> Commit a Scripture verse to memory and use it as your mantra when you are tempted. The Word of God is alive and life changing! In the 40-day temptation of Christ, He came back with Scripture when He was tempted.

2. Our fantasies could be about the desire of our souls for a different outcome to a previous failure, loss, or reversal in life. Loss comes in many different packages for us men, and they are hard to talk about. Some men experienced losses in life that still haunt them into adulthood. How many of us men have longed for a different outcome with the final touchdown throw, the final tackle to save a win, the shot at the buzzer, the last at bat, the goal with seconds left, the ace to win it all. Winning it all is every man's dream. We would ask you: Does this same desire for a different outcome haunt your sexual fantasies? Do you long for a girlfriend who does not leave you? A prom queen who doesn't leave the dance with someone else? A class beauty who doesn't break off your short-lived relationship? A wife who comes back home?

Are your sexual fantasies revealing a broken heart that has never been healed, a broken heart that longs for a different outcome? A classical male response here: "I don't want to think or talk about it." Do you get the picture? Is there an emotional healing that you need, and is it being revealed by your fantasies?

3. For some of us, our sexual fantasies are about a love-hunger that is an all-consuming idolatry. A client named Tony told us about a break-up with a particular girlfriend that was more painful than any other. Their relationship had been a lot of fun and also had included several evenings of passionate kissing in full embrace. There was no sex, not even any petting, just full embraces, mouth to mouth. After she broke up with him, Tony was devastated and lonely. It didn't make sense to him. When he fantasized of being with her again, he would relive the memories of their nights of passionate kissing. When pressed about his fantasies of her, he stopped mid sentence. He looked at the ground with pain and bewilderment. He so desperately wanted to figure out why there was such a consuming obsession in his heart regarding this girl. Then he said, "When I think of holding her and kissing her, it's like she completed me. I can't release her. Can't get her out of my mind. And it's been going on for a long time." He had lost his sense of self.

As believers, we hold to the truth that we are complete in Christ. Our loving Savior abides in us, and we are complete in Him. If we start to believe that we need a woman or sexual experience to complete ourselves, we have fallen for a lie! Remember John 15, where Jesus says, "Abide in Me, and I in you." No woman can meet the deepest longing of a man's soul; only God can do that.

The truth is, Tony's trying to follow his past girlfriend around like a lost puppy is only driving her farther and farther away. His was a knock-off of love that was obsessive at best and idolatry at worst, and the roller coaster left Tony emotionally and spiritually incapacitated. He was crippled by his desire. His fantasies were the clue.

If, in your fantasies, your desire for "the Woman" is a devouring, all-consuming enmeshing of your identities into an adrenaline-charged, dopamine-norapinephrine spike of sexual ecstasy, then—wow!—you are definitely in a fantasy. But the heart of your longing is evident. You have a deep spiritual need that you are trying to fulfill in this ecstasy.

4. Your fantasies can simply be the conditioning of our culture, our highly charged culture of glamorous romance and sex. Everywhere we look, we are bombarded with images of the rich, the famous, the beautiful, the stars. From television to the magazine racks at the checkout line, or online at the bottom of every page, it's all steamy, oozing with sexual innuendo. Everyone is dressing sexy, going on sexy vacations, showing off perfect bikini bodies, groping and kissing in the surf. The message is, "that's what life is all about," and you need to get in on the action.

A pattern develops. We can think the stars have it. We don't. We want it. We can't have it, so we fantasize that we do. Stories flood into our minds. Our sexual fantasies can be charged with the images we picked up during the day. Those who have come of age in this generation have been so bombarded with sex and lust presented as romance and love that they have the concepts wedded together. Increasingly, even in the church, this generation of young people feels that sex is a rite of passage. "Our parents say they waited to have sex until they were married. That seems impossible. Life must have been completely different." Research shows that more than 60 percent of all single Christians ages 18-59, when asked if they would have sex before marriage, said Yes.[27]

Our sexual fantasies today can be manufactured out of the jealousy, envy, emptiness, and longing to catch up to the culture and have the kind of sex that we keep being told is ubiquitous in our world. God says something different. And many young men and women are still desiring to stay pure till marriage.

---

27 Kenny Luck, "The Deadly Deception of Sexual Atheism in the Church, *Charisma Magazine,* Oct. 7, 2014 (http://www.charismamag.com/life/relationships/20385-the-deadly-deception-of -sexual-atheism-in-the-church)(Accessed December 24, 2014).

TAKING YOUR FANTASIES CAPTIVE TO CHRIST

If we will analyze our sexual fantasies, confess them for what they are, repent, and seek to turn from these ways, we can ask God how He can help us be set free from them. Work hard to understand that the cry of your soul is sending a message to your heart. These messages are about youth, loneliness, first longings, first loves, and first losses. Your soul has been longing to be deeply loved and accepted. The *old pain* in your heart will often drive you back to the *old ways* that you once used to comfort that old pain.

When you discern the message that your soul is sending you, then you can take that message to Christ, and learn His truth on the matter.

Let's summarize where we have come in this chapter: Apart from expressing oneness with your wife, your inappropriate sexual fantasy can be an attempt to capture some form of acceptance, affirmation, nurturing, power, or control; it is often a symbolic way of seeking to comfort or resolve your emotional needs. But these ways of thinking, though entrenched in the brain, can be rewired. Your mind can be renewed.

Your fantasies can be your teachers, guiding you to greater emotional, mental, and spiritual health. To do this, we suggest asking these revealing questions about your fantasies:

1. *Who* are the people in your fantasy? Is it the Playboy centerfold? Is she a particular face and body from an Internet porn site? Is she an old girlfriend, or an old crush? Is it the person who abandoned you? Is it the person who broke your heart? Is it someone you actually are angry with? Is it someone who seems to love you and treat you the way you have always wanted to be treated? Oftentimes the person being objectified in your fantasies is someone related to your first love or your first sexual experience. Sometimes, the particular kind of body you look for in pornography has the same kind of body that enraptured you at an early age when you saw porn for the very first time.

2. *What* do they say? Do they tell you to stay: "Don't leave"? Do they tell you they love you? Do they tell you that you are amazing? Based on their words and actions, what are they saying about you? The answer to this question will be revealing, for it will tell you what you have been longing to hear all your life (e.g., that you are wanted, that you are handsome, that you are adequate, that you are a hero, you protected her, saved her, etc.). What you hear is the story you have wanted to hear. Write it down when it reveals itself to you.

3. *Where* does your fantasy take place? Is it in old familiar places? Do you return to the scene of first love? To the scene of broken trust? To the scene of lost virginity? To the scene of great sexual power? This is the question that leads you to discover that you are trying to imagine a familiar place but often with a different result, so as to redo the emotional impact of that memory. Again, let your memory speak to you. Let it tell you what might be unfinished in the story.

4. Finally, *what happens* in your fantasy? Is it a real memory that you are building from? Is it a brand-new scene? Do you arrive some place you did not arrive in a real memory? Do you achieve something you did not achieve in the real memory? Do you get the kiss, the acceptance, the sexual experience, the love that you did not get in real life? What kind of emotions do you feel as the scene unfolds? What kind of state does it leave you in?

The point of asking these questions is to help allow your fantasies to teach you, so you can renew your mind in regard to that message. It is like the "great and powerful Oz" being revealed—once the truth is seen, the fantasy's power starts to be taken away. Your sexual behavior is not typically because you get "horny," and so you always go to lust, pornography and self-gratification! No, your sexual behavior could be telling you something about yourself you need to know, just as your aggressiveness in business is telling you something you need to know, and your neat-freak-controlling of things at home is telling you something you need to know, and your yelling and screaming in traffic is telling you something you need to know.

Your sexual acts can reveal that something is missing in your life. Your particular choice of pornography is revealing another dimension to that which is missing. You can blow this off, and close the book and say, "You guys are crazy. I look at porn because I'm a guy. Period." And, sadly, you can keep getting lost in that world of fantasy for the rest of your life, and never have satisfying intimacy and purity with your wife. You can be frustrated and angry; and one day your granddaughters will turn away from you when your hugs make them feel uncomfortable. And you will be lonely.

Or you can say, "I'm in. I'm going to do this exercise and I'm going to see what God will do when He meets me in my fantasies and delivers me from them." Yes, we are encouraging you not to look at your fantasies to get triggered again. We are encouraging you to take Christ into your fantasies. Take Him there and let Him capture your thoughts, your rationalizations, your victim attitudes, your hurts and losses, and take it all with Him to the cross, and exchange it for His healing presence. His healing will rewire your brain.

Now that you have a deeper understanding of the battle, here are some things you can do to man up to the challenge:

1. Allow Him to teach you that those women are His daughters.

2. Learn to see Her (your wife or girlfriend) in her beauty. Look into her eyes. Enjoy her laughter, wit, wisdom. Be nourished in her love.

3. Learn to participate in non-sensual touch. Build intimacy with her.

4. Love her; don't use her.

5.   Married men: Make your wife the heart of your fantasy and your thought life.

Our fantasies and self-serving sex are our attempts to get our needs met in our own way. It's actually a false attempt at loving ourselves. It's not very loving, though, is it? How many of you would do the following? If your young son came home from school with a long face, and told you that he had been picked on, or that his girlfriend left school with another boy, or that he had flunked a test, how many of you men would invite your son into the computer room and say, "Son, I know you're feeling down, so ol' dad is going to show you how to feel better." How many of you would stand above your son seated at the computer, and show him how to find pornography, and how to feel better? "What? Of course, not!" you say. "That would not be the loving thing to do at all!"

Then why do you do it to yourself?

Why have you done it to yourself for all of these years?

When are you going to love yourself and do whatever it takes to fight for the grace of God to deliver you?

Understand that your sexual longings and fantasies are messages from your soul.

Analyze the scenes and story lines, and allow them to reveal to you the earlier memory on which they are built, and the earlier longing that they were created to heal.

Learn the messages that you discover in your analysis. Learn the "thoughts and imaginations" that the fantasies are built on. (See Second Corinthians 10:4-5.)

Take these thoughts and imaginations into the healing presence of Christ, and let Him replace them with His love, His truth, His comfort, His encouragement for you.

Let Him renew your mind through the washing of the Word. Let your brain be rewired, as you think His new thoughts about yourself and your identity, replacing your old thoughts that only made you feel unloved and empty. We are going to teach you more on how to do this in later chapters.

And don't do this alone. Seek out men in your life who will regularly remind you of truth and who will stand with you. This is what real accountability is about, other men who constantly "bombard" you with love, friendship and God's truth. Most of us at times will need to find the love, nurture, affirmation, attention, and blessing in our relationships with other men. You need these relationships the most if you never felt that your father affirmed, loved, or blessed you (or if your mother didn't either). This healthy love you long for will never arrive in your heart from some fantasy. But it can come through real relationships with real men today! David said his friendship with Jonathan was greater than the love of a woman to him (see Second Samuel 1:26).

God's love is redemptive, powerful, exhilarating, and freeing. His love is strong. Instead of trying to hide this area of your life from your walk with Him, allow Him to show you how to use His strength in this battle. Ask Him to help you love your wife and male friends with a strong love, and ask Him to help you accept healthy love and friendship in return.

Let God love you better than all of these sexual fantasies ever did.

Let God help you to see the love of your life as His gift to you, to love and be loved. Enjoy her.

Let God love you through some powerful relationships with other men.

It begins to change everything.

QUESTIONS FOR REFLECTION OR DISCUSSION

1. In your private journal, start to answer the four questions posed in this chapter for analyzing fantasies. This could be the most important work you do on the journey to freedom. More than likely this will take weeks and weeks of reflection and prayer. Start now. Ask the Holy Spirit to teach you about your fantasies. Be honest. Receive. Do not minimize or rationalize what you hear.

2. As you do this work, begin also to write out new prayers, new thoughts about sex, marriage and purity that emerge in your heart.

3. Develop your network of men friends. Do you have any older men in your life, or in your church, who can be encouragers in this journey?

Throughout the next several chapters, we will teach you the following exercises to help you guard your heart and mind:

1. Thought Stopping
2. Thought Replacement
3. Training my Eyes
4. Intimacy Building

5

BUILDING BLOCKS OF STRONGHOLDS

*Flee from sexual immorality. All other sins a
man commits are outside the body, but he who
sins sexually sins against his own body.*

—1 CORINTHIANS 6:18

When I (Tim) grew up in Pennsylvania, I had a great backdrop for growing up as a boy. A dirt road led two miles to an old rented farmhouse.
Large family. Fishing, hunting. An old '69 2+2 Fastback Mustang. A lot
of fun.

The long dirt lane that led from the dirt road to our home ran alongside a small farm stream. But every spring, we had a problem. With a
season of rain would come the yellow clay mud that filled the heart of our
lane and turned into nastier mud. We would get stuck constantly, even
to the point of "saddle-bagging" the cars. My brother Tom and I worked

endless hours with our dad trying to put shale and boards down to build a base and fix the problem. It never worked. The shale would disappear in the mud. Every time we drove up or down that road, ruts would form and even go deeper and deeper. We had a foundation problem. When the weather would dry, the mud would clear up, and it seemed to be all gone. But it wasn't.

The fight of your life is like that. Patterns emerge and begin to sink deep into your heart and soul and your way of life. They devour your best intentions. It's as persistent as tar or grease on your body, which as you may know doesn't come off easily. If it's hot, it will continue to burn until it's cooled or removed. Sexual sin is like that. It's tough stuff to scrub out. It might not be on your hands, but it's on your heart.

Strongholds are stubborn challenges. Just as athletes train their bodies to have muscle memory to compete at the highest level, accordingly a man's mind can be trained toward lust, so much so that it can become a stronghold. And it's tough to break free. Real tough!

How does a man end up with a stronghold in his life? The simple answer is: repetition over time. There are specific "building-block behaviors" that link together to develop a fairly predictable foundation or pattern on which a stronghold develops. These strongholds often begin early in a person's life. In general, the earlier the building blocks are in place, the more likely that a stronghold will result.

Take a look at these building blocks. Which of them may have come into your life?

Building Block #1: Deep Emotional and Spiritual Longings

Every man has needs, emotional, relational, and spiritual, even if he acts as if he doesn't. He does. Virtually every man also has a degree of a sexual appetite. As humans we are made to deeply desire connection, touch, worthiness, value, and acceptance—words we readily associate with genuine and unconditional love. We want to be loved, not because of anything we achieve or accomplish, but solely on the basis of the truth that we are created by God and valued by God. To put it a better way: Every kid needs someone in life who is crazy about him or her.

Unfortunately, many boys are not raised with these essential needs met. They receive more criticism than praise, are not appropriately touched with affection, and do not have security woven into their understanding of life. Children who are denied these things from their parents do not lose their desire for these things—but they do go elsewhere to get affirmation and signs of acceptance.

Thus was the case for Billy. Like most young boys, Billy loved his father and had a deep desire to emulate him. Dad was strong, in charge, and mostly inaccessible. Nevertheless, Dad was Billy's hero. There were days when Dad had no time for Billy, and he might not even be home for dinner in the evenings. Dad's infrequent appearance in Billy's daily life supercharged the meaning of their infrequent times together, and when Dad was short or impatient with Billy, it hurt deeply, even into Billy's teen years.

Billy sought to regain those feelings of closeness and affirmation through multiple sexual encounters in his teen years. The moments of feeling "loved" and valued were fleeting, both in the giving and receiving. Even so, the sexual pleasure became a deep inner drive, however fleeting the pleasure may be.

Billy had been "set up" for a sexual stronghold by empty parenting. His past hurts were deep, yet he had pushed away his true longings as a defense mechanism.

> Every man who knocks on the door of a brothel is looking for God.
> —G. K. CHESTERTON

In their book, *The Sacred Romance,* authors Brent Curtis and John Eldredge talk about the arrows that pierce us.[28] We feel the sting of rejec-

---

28   Brent Curtis and John Eldredge, *The Sacred Romance: Drawing Closer to the Heart of God* (Nashville: Thomas Nelson, 1997).

tion from a peer, or we receive a message from Dad that we don't measure up and are unloved or unworthy. The pain can cut deep. Every person feels the arrows of relationship wounds in his or her lifetime. We deal with the hurt in different ways, but sometimes we create walls and try to deny our emotional and spiritual needs.

The result can be deep emotional and spiritual longings that are not being filled through a relationship with Christ. Sometimes men do not turn to Christ to fill the longings because they fail to acknowledge that the longings are there, so they reach for anything to anesthetize the pain and the emptiness. Is it any wonder then that Sunday is the most popular day to view porn?[29]

STRATEGY
Sit down and write out a plan for how you will continue to be filled spiritually. Include quiet time, church, worship music, and any retreats or conferences that could speak to you.

Building Block #2: Sexual Fantasy

The second building block for sexual addiction is sexual fantasy. Sexual fantasy is simply thinking about sex. Normal people think about sex, and fantasy is not necessarily unhealthful or wrong. If you are married, you might have thoughts about spending some alone time this weekend when your kids are sleeping over at their grandparents'. You might be looking forward to a honeymoon with your fiancée. These are examples of healthy anticipation of a gift God intends for you to enjoy.

The building block of a sexual stronghold comes when the thoughts of sex begin to happen with more and more frequency—and the fantasies

---

29   From Covenant Eyes: Porn Stats (http://www.covenanteyes.com/2010/06/16/porn-stats -most-popular-day-to-watch-porn-is-sunday/) (Accessed February 5, 2015).

are about behavior that is sinful. A beautiful woman who walks by, and you undress her mentally. You wonder for a fleeting moment what it would be like to spend a night with your best friend's knockout new girlfriend. You run into the bank to cash a check and let your imagination get carried away when an attractive young teller gives you a flirty smile.

Fantasies in themselves are not our enemy. Fantasies are mental pictures, images, and stories that a person creates—perhaps not consciously as if he or she is writing a novel, but created in the mind nonetheless. What a person cuts and pastes together in his or her mind is what that person *wishes* had happened or might happen.

In many cases, fantasies are motivating for a person, and often in a positive way. We may call our fantasies "dreams." We dream of a better life, and then begin to pursue it with goals, a plan, and even specific entries scribbled into our planners. Those who have strong dreams that they believe are God-given callings usually discuss their dreams with God in their prayers.

In other cases, however, fantasies can motivate a person in a negative way. The fantasies become what the Bible calls "lusts." Three main lusts can be identified in Scripture: the lust of the flesh (including sexual lust, gluttony, and anything else that seeks to satisfy a physical craving), the lust of the eyes (generally identified as a craving for possessions or greed), and the pride of life (a strong desire for power, fame, and having things "our" way). Lusts can set a person on a track toward goal making, plan engineering, and scheduling. They drive people toward accomplishing their lusts. Rarely, however, do people seek God's help in achieving their lustful pursuits. Why? Because they intuitively and spiritually know that their lusts are at least partially contrary to God's highest and best plan.

A person with intense fantasies that are contrary to God's commandments is often filled with guilt, even "before the fact" of any outward behavior. Although the person may not always recognize it as such, the main reason is that the person is fantasizing something that is a substitute for God's blessing, love, nurture, or affirmation.

In a sexual fantasy, the person who is the object of the fantasy has all of the stuff that the fantasizer desires. The object may be a person from the past, perhaps an old high school sweetheart, or a movie or TV star, or even a composite person constructed from people that the fantasizer knows. These imaginary lovers never say "no" to an invitation for sex. They are always willing. And they never let you down.

Men stuck in this cycle are often unconsciously aware that their fantasy affirmation is a cheap knock off of the real deal, but instead of turning away, they become more and more entrenched in seeking to imagine the perfect fantasy.

We will talk more about these fantasies throughout this book—where they come from, what they can teach you, and how to stop the thoughts you do not want. For now, know that entertaining mental images of sinful sexual behavior is a building block for a sexual stronghold.

Building Block #3: Pornography

Michelangelo wasn't talking about pornography when he said "Everything is created twice: first in the mind, and then in reality," but boy, does it apply! For most men, what begins in fantasy takes on visual reality in the form of photos and movies. This is the third building block for sexual addiction.

Defining pornography is not an easy task. If pornography is defined simply as a display of nudity, then many galleries in many museums would be off-limits. At the other end of the spectrum, there are dialogues on television that display no nudity and do not even describe sexual acts, but nonetheless are sexually suggestive and are set up to bring explicit sexual imagery into a person's mind.

The technical definition still accepted by many is that pornography is writing about or displaying by some medium (magazines, videos, movies, the Internet) nudity or sexual activity that excites sexual feelings. For the Christian man, we might extend our definition to add, "that excite unhealthful, immoral, and sinful sexual feelings and entice someone to sexual behavior."

The ultimate determining factor as to whether something is pornographic does not lie in the visual images themselves, but rather in what begins to happen in your mind, how an image or sequence of images triggers a person to act out sexual fantasies. Porn gives the addict a focus for his fantasy: It identifies for the addict a potential partner in the fantasy and a potential methodology for engaging in sex with that "virtual" partner. At the same time, it fuels an increased passion for sex that demands release.

What is pornographic to one man may not be considered pornographic to another. Keep this in mind as we talk later about accountability—you will need someone who you can talk with about your personal triggers and how to avoid them. As men, we need to be aware of our own lusts and identify material that enflames those lusts.

For our purposes here, we will regard pornography as sexually explicit material that dehumanizes, objectifies, and degrades men and women for the purpose of sexual arousal and gratification.

Porn is everywhere.

Porn sites attract more visitors on the Internet each month than Twitter, Amazon, and Netflix *combined*. But, there is a dichotomy going on with the porn industry. The porn industry is both gaining more and more acceptability in mainstream culture while we are at the same time learning more and more about the genuinely harmful nature of pornographic material.

Today, pornographic material and subjects do not carry the same taboo within mainstream culture as they previously did. Some see porn as "informative." Some see it as "entertaining" and some even view it as "healthy." Few see the truth—how damaging it is.

One study reported that two-thirds of all Christ-professing men have visited Internet porn sites and struggle with memories of what they have seen there.[30] An increasing number of women are accessing Internet pornography, and it has become everyone's problem.[31]

Psychologist Al Cooper has written extensively on Internet addictions and he describes three factors that he calls the Triple-A Engines.[32] Accessible, Affordable, and Anonymous. *Accessible:* Just about anybody with a computer or smartphone can access pornography. *Affordable:* The free pornographic material is so extensive that a person could spend days, weeks, and even months looking at free material. An estimated 90 percent of pornography on the Internet is free![33] *Anonymous:* With the privacy of Internet access in the home or anywhere with Wi-Fi, there is no shame as there would be with purchasing pornographic material in a store.

Prolonged exposure to pornography creates and enhances sexual callousness toward women, including a loss of respect for a women's sexual autonomy and her right to the privacy of her own body. It also distorts the view of how men behave sexually. This loss of respect frequently turns into a diminished capacity to relate to women in a mutually fulfilling, healthy manner. Pornography can perpetuate a cycle of loneliness, because it attempts to replace true intimacy while harming the viewer's ability to be intimate.

Dave was 13 years old when he first saw pornography. A friend had stolen the magazine from the local drug store. Dave never forgot what he saw in those pages: a fully nude centerfold. Dave's adolescent hormones were running wild, and he had a powerful electric feeling that was both physical and emotional. The woman in the magazine was smiling and seemed to be looking right at Dave, as if she wanted him to look at her.

---

30 Proven Men Ministries, with the Barna Group, 2014 Pornography Survey and Statistics (http://www.provenmen.org/2014pornsurvey)(Accessed February 5, 2015).

31 Dannah Gresh and Juli Slattery, *Pulling Back the Shades: Erotica, Intimacy and the Longings of a Woman's Heart* (Chicago, Moody: 2014).

32 Al Cooper, *Sex and the Internet: A guidebook for clinicians* (New York: Brunner-Routledge, 2000).

33 From Josh McDowell, "Just1ClickAway" (http://www.just1clickaway.org/)(Accessed February 5, 2015).

She seemed to be enjoying the fact that she was being admired. Dave saw in her someone who answered the loneliness in his own soul.

At 13, Dave wondered if any girl like that would ever like him. He was not unusual in that respect. He had insecurities about how much his mother did or didn't like him. His mother rarely smiled and was not good at emotional connection.

Sadly, without open communication with older men and accountability partners about sexuality, Dave turned to pornography to define his understanding of sexuality and women, and he continued to do so for the next two decades. Pornographic sites and magazines told Dave that women always enjoy sex and never say no. They perform sexual acts without ever being disgusted or insecure. They enjoy making men feel good. Women exist for men's pleasure. Men are consumers of this commodity, taking without giving, and engaging in sex without true intimacy.

There was no one at home, at school, or at church talking about sex and correcting the misperceptions that pornography had put in place. An unseen, twisted magazine editor was the "older and wiser" person leading the way, and also leading him astray.

By the time Dave was in his early thirties, his expectations were so warped that there was no way any woman would ever really satisfy him in the real world. His young beautiful wife didn't have a chance against the "professionals" that had been in Dave's mind over the years. This is how, as a married man, Dave found himself still feeling that he "needed" pornography. Sounds like bondage turned into to a stronghold.

The person who tends to live in a fantasy world, or at least resort to fantasies often, tends to be a person who is lonely, tired, anxious, deeply wounded, or sad—usually a combination of these traits. If you're soaking up porn, you may not even be able to pinpoint exactly why you are feeling some of those things.

Building Block #4: Shame

At the heart of sexual sin is shame. Let's be honest about something, frankly honest. We *think* that our sexual sins started in our preteen years.

We think this because that is when it came with such a powerful force into our lives. When we were in our preteen years, we were goggle-eyed fascinated with the vision of a naked woman, who, in our mind's eye, undressed and revealed the glory of her nakedness to us.

But this is not where the story of sex insanity started. Let's go back to the Garden of Eden for a moment. Genesis 2 ends with Adam and Eve standing peacefully in nakedness before one another. The closing scene is described this way. "And the man and his wife were both naked and not ashamed" (Genesis 2:25, ESV).

There was no shame to be naked in each other's presence or in the presence of God. Adam was comfortable in his own skin, and Eve in hers. God's design for marriage was this: "naked and not ashamed."

Remember that anything with that much propensity for beauty has that much propensity for pain. Hell is against anything that smacks of righteousness. Your sexuality is not above the target of Hell, so the enemy comes lurking. He comes to steal, kill and destroy that Garden of Eden oneness.

"Naked" gave way to "covering up." "Not ashamed" gave way to "hiding and fear." When Adam and Eve ate from the wrong tree, "the eyes of both were opened, and they knew that they were naked. And they sewed fig leaves together and made themselves loincloths" (Genesis 3:7, ESV). The man and the woman lost their identity of naked *oneness*. They felt alienated from and even fearful of one another and God, and so they covered up and hid—first from each other, then from God.

Enter shame. *Shame is the inability to accept yourself and find comfort in your own skin.* It involves that "deep sense that you are unacceptable because of something you did, something done to you, or something associated with you."[34]

There is a threefold result of shame: devaluing, "smallness," and hiding. Shame is shot through with fear.

---

34 Ed Welch, *Shame Interrupted* (Greensboro, N.C.: New Growth Press, 2012), 2.

We have this instinctive need for acceptance in the deepest part of our being. We want to be wanted. We want to be admired. We want to be acceptable.

Shame grows when a mother scolds a child for misbehaving with, "Shame on you; God is going to punish you!" Shame grows when you are screamed at for spilling, dropping, breaking, or knocking over something, or when your little playmates made fun of you for being too chubby, too skinny, too freckled, or too ugly. Children are told at home and at play that they are not acceptable, not admired, not wanted.

Shame is about me as a person. It gives birth to an identity. As I get older, shame often becomes the master of my slavery to sexual sin. My shame drives me to find comfort, and the enemy makes sure that sexual fantasy is offered as that comfort. And for those who went to Sunday school, oh my, you got filled with the self-condemning shame of being so despicable and dirty. For sure, God did not like the things you did and thought in secret. You were going to go to church on Sunday, but He wasn't going to get a chance to look you in the eye! You were hiding, self-condemning, unapproved, and a disappointment. You were despicable, even dirty. Unacceptable. You carried secrets, secrets, and more secrets. Shame became an identity.

When hurtful, painful events happen in our lives, we try to make meaning out of them. Before he got to the summer camp, Richard had decided in his heart that being skinny made him unworthy and unacceptable, and he hated how God had made him. His identity was being formed in self-rejection. For Richard, shame was a nametag on his chest that read: "Unworthy." His beliefs about himself were, "I am skinny and powerless. I will never be good enough. I will always lose out in life. God has failed me by making me skinny. Love (and therefore, sex) will always be scarce." These thoughts in his mind produced emotions of pain, anger, and fear. Now Richard needed relief, and shame would introduce him to our second, internal battle—the fight with his flesh.

Our shame is lived out in "the flesh." Our shame drives behaviors that we call "the flesh." This word appears all over the Bible, and most often it is referring, of course, to human bodies. However, in a few instances Paul is not referring to the human body when he uses this term. In these few instances he is referring to a coping strategy, a mind-set, an ungodly way of living that flows from an ungodly way of thinking.

The flesh is my strategy for living out of my own resources (see Galatians 6:8). It is how I live independently from God in my own coping patterns of self-sufficiency (see Romans 8:5-8). The flesh is a mind-set, if you will, a pattern of operating, by which I trust myself to meet my needs, instead of trusting God with my needs (see Galatians 5:19). When I "walk according to the flesh":

I *protect* myself,

I *provide* for myself,

I *pleasure* myself,

I *promote* myself.

When I do all of this apart from God it's called "the flesh."

When a man is walking in sexual sins outside of the will of God, he is living according to the flesh. Shame often drives him there. He will protect himself and lie about his secrets. He will provide for himself and lie to get sex. He will lust and pleasure himself if he's lonely, instead of praying to God. He will brag and manipulate to promote himself. He will posture and pose. He will act all phony and self-righteous. His shame will drive him to do all this apart from God—all to get acceptance, to get the love, the girl, the sex that he thinks acting like that will provide!

Shame differs from conviction. Conviction occurs when a man recognizes that he has disobeyed God and the man is filled with godly sorrow and repentance. Paul wrote: "Godly sorrow brings repentance that leads to salvation and leaves no regret, but worldly sorrow brings death" (2 Corinthians 7:10).

Shame is feeling bad about our personhood, or who we are. Conviction refers to knowing or thinking we have done something wrong.[35] Shame fuels the flesh and guilt fuels the shame.

> *For the desires of the flesh are against the Spirit, and the desires of the Spirit are against the flesh, for these are opposed to each other, to keep you from doing the things you want to do* (Galatians 5:17, ESV).

Do you see that last line? There is a life of sexual purity that God has called us to live, but the flesh keeps us from doing it. The flesh and the Spirit are at war with each other. No wonder there is a sexual battle! No wonder it's so hard on our hearts. Our new heart, created in Christ Jesus, wants to walk in step with the Holy Spirit. But what the flesh desires is relief from shame through sexual gratification, self-indulgence, a quick fix. But this not what the Spirit wants. When a man's body gets electrically and chemically charged up by fantasies or pornography and his mind is overwhelmed with shame, then he will yield to the habits of the flesh, and fall away from purity with overwhelming guilt! Then, of course, shame grows even more.

Shame grows as sexual failures mount.

Shame opens the door to deep emotional pain such as anxiety, fear, emptiness and loneliness. These are the strong shame-based emotions that escort young boys into the world of lust and self-sex.

Do you like emotional pain? You don't. You want relief.

Shame drives us to find relief. So, a vicious cycle starts up. We look for comfort in what? In the elusive intimacy of imaginations in our minds, with more false intimacy of pornography, maybe sex with girls in school, or—when we get older—in the illicit intimacy of an affair. We have the false belief that satisfying this craving, somehow, is going to heal something inside; we think that sex is going to bring us acceptance and

---

35 From Covenant Eyes, 2013, "Guilt vs. Shame: Why Definitions Matter" (http://www .covenanteyes.com/2013/02/01/guilt-vs-shame-why-definitions-matter/)(Accessed February 5, 2015).

affirmation, the healing of our fear, anxiety and loneliness. Instead of comfort, it only increases sexual brokenness and shame, which leads to even more aloneness.

Shame is like kryptonite. It vaporizes our power. It devalues us. Without purity in our hearts, we have no power for this battle. Sexual sin strips a man of integrity and power.

Shame causes men to hide. When we hide, we fight alone. We look for help, alone. We look at pornography, alone. We lose the battle, alone. We go to church and cover up. Alone. What did God say in the Garden? "It is not good for man to be alone."

Shame makes a man shrink away in silence, and one of the greatest enemies of sexual health and purity is silence. In a sense, we are dying inside because we do not like to talk about our pain, our anger, or our fear.

Freedom comes by exchanging your identity.

Disaster can be averted by putting on the Lord Jesus Christ and making no provision for the flesh to gratify its desires (see Romans 13:14). We fight for our purity when we don't let shame and the flesh have dominion. We stay in the fight when we live in our true identity, in the Spirit of life in Christ Jesus (see Romans 8:2), and are controlled by the Holy Spirit (see Ephesians 5:18). The battle calls for readiness. Shame-based thinking and physical, bodily senses are going to be triggered often. Each day, I need to set my heart and mind in my new identity in Christ. I need to quit playing defense and line up on offense!

Building Block #5: Self-Sex

The fifth building block of sexual addiction is self-sex. Regular, frequent, habitual viewing of pornography nearly always leads to masturbation. This activity often begins with natural childhood curiosity. Normal exploration, however, is not what we are talking about here.

Ted grew up with ADD (attention deficit disorder) and probably also HD (hyperactivity disorder). Typical of children with these disorders, he had a hard time turning off both his body and his mind, which continually seemed to be racing and always posed for action.

When he was a preteen, he often had difficulty going to sleep at night. He would lie in bed wishing for his mother to come in, comfort him, and perhaps give him a back rub to calm him down. His mother, however, never showed up to do these things. She didn't know he needed her, and she was tired and stressed, too.

One evening, Ted discovered that he could create the desired calming effect by messing with himself, and especially as he touched his genitals. As he entered adolescence, this pattern resulted in masturbation, eventually as a nightly ritual. He found he couldn't go to sleep until he had masturbated, and eventually this "need" led him to look at pornography, which he discovered could help him reach an arousal state.

Years later, after he was married, he still had trouble sleeping, and he frequently left the bed he shared with his wife and went to another part of the house to look at porn and have self-sex.

One night, his wife got up and went downstairs in search of her husband and discovered what was going on. You know the rest of the story.

In Ted's case, the need for physical touch and intimacy had led him to masturbate, and it was masturbation that led to pornography. For a greater percentage of those who deal with sexual strongholds, the process happens in reverse. They have the need for physical intimacy, and this leads them to seek a substitute provider for that intimacy, usually a voluptuous, seemingly caring woman staring out at him from a magazine photograph or an Internet image. The feelings of arousal build up to a perceived "need" for masturbation.

The overarching principle here is that masturbation always involves sexual thoughts and fantasies, which are inevitably linked to the visual image of someone. The person may be unknown—for example, the person in a video or porn magazine—or the fantasy may involve someone who is known, past or present. The desire that fuels the lust, which leads to sexual arousal, is nearly always personified. If the person being imagined is not a spouse, then the entire activity falls into the categories of adultery or fornication, which are sins expressly addressed by Jesus.

Jesus taught that sin does not need to be a physical experience; it can be a forbidden mental/emotional experience. He said, "everyone who looks at a woman with lust for her has already committed adultery with her in his heart" (Matthew 5:28, NASB). The Bible makes it clear that God looks upon the heart and knows the heart of every person.

The Bible as a whole presents sexual behavior in the contexts of commitment, fidelity, and a concern with showing respect for one's spouse. This includes spiritual and emotional communication and mutual support, as well as material provision and protection. Even the person who masturbates to fantasies of the spouse, but who regards sexual intimacy as something apart from a total spiritual and emotional connection, is in a state of sin and is falling far short of God's ideal.

Building Block #6: Infidelity

There is a fifth foundation stone to a sexual stronghold which is a part of some men's lives—the pursuit of sexual affairs with real-life people who are outside the boundaries of marriage.

By the time Frank married in his early twenties, he had several women with whom he had engaged in sexual intercourse. He did not regard himself as "promiscuous" but preferred to think of himself as "experienced."

In looking back over his childhood, Frank had very few happy memories of time spent with his family. Mom and Dad seemed to be warring constantly over one thing or another—overspending the family budget, overdrinking at the local bar, arguing over acts of inconsiderate behavior. There were no bedtime prayers or goodnight kisses from either parent in all of Frank's memory.

Frank could not have described or defined the ache inside him, but years later, he regarded it as a "need" to feel close to somebody, to have a sense that he mattered to someone and that the person really mattered to him in return.

His best friend, Gordon, as an 11-year-old told him the facts about sex. Frank wanted to know more and Gordon subsequently introduced him to a secret cache of magazines that he had hidden in a box under his bed and a couple of online sites. Frank began to fantasize about being held close and in a loving way by the women in these magazines. And when Gordon's supply of visual images had been thoroughly committed to memory, Frank began to get lost in his own world of porn.

It was only a small step for Frank to take in seeking out a sexual partner. He was only 15, but inwardly felt as if he was 25, when a pretty and voluptuous eighteen-year-old girl found him "amusing" at an amusement park. She became his partner for his first sexual experience in the dark shadows behind the tilt-a-whirl ride. She took him to Mars and back. He was emboldened by that experience and soon began to flirt with girls closer to his age, who found his sexual knowledge greater than theirs and his charming ways difficult to resist.

For all of his experience, however, Frank did not feel "satisfied." The longing he had to feel close to someone, to be truly and deeply loved by a person, remained. He figured that need might only be met fully if he was married to someone who promised to love him, and with whom he might have sex as often as he wanted it.

Enter Louise, when he was 20. Within six months, Frank decided that she would be a wonderful mother for his children someday, a faithful wife, and a willing sex partner. They married and things were good for a few months. Then, Frank's insatiable appetite for sex—insatiable from Louise's perspective—led Louise to say, "I have a headache" as she rolled over and went to sleep rather than yield to his kisses and caresses.

Frank felt rejected, rebuffed, and angry. After several of these experiences, Frank crawled out of bed one night and went downstairs to "do a little work." He had only been signed on to his Internet account for about 15 minutes when he veered onto a site that promised to provide far more stimulation than *Playboy* ever had.

And thus began a nightly 2:00 A.M. habit of watching Internet porn, masturbating, and then returning to his bed to sleep. The nightly ritual gave Frank some sexual release, but also caused a great deal of guilt. He had a feeling that he was "cheating" on Louise. He also felt angry at her for denying him the sexual fulfillment he desired, and angry at himself for feeling angry with her. It was a vicious emotional and behavioral cycle.

Within months, Frank had found Kassy at the bar of a hotel in a nearby town, and she became his periodic lover. Soon after, Connie was discovered as a lonely new-in-town waitress at Frank's favorite diner, and she too, became a part-time lover. Frank found it a little exciting that Louise and Kassy and Connie might encounter one another but never seemed to cross paths. And even if they did, he reasoned, he still had the "girls" on the Internet to supply him with sexual gratification.

Frank is far from an isolated case when it comes to having multiple affairs in progress at any given time. It seems like broken boundaries in this realm just snowball; even when the man feels shame and regret, the behavior often continues. Countless men have developed deep emotional ties with their mistresses, and catch this—while still claiming to "love" their wives.

It should also be noted that even a one-time encounter can be regarded as an affair. Sexual messages are so rampant in our world today that a general assumption in our society seems to be that all people have sex before marriage, and that certain casual encounters are not really affairs, only forms of "having fun." Indeed, fornication has become casually known in our world today as "friends with benefits." We need to be clear: Sex with a person outside the parameters of marriage is against God's commandments regarding sexual purity and marriage fidelity.

Unmet emotional needs are not met by masturbation or by affairs. They are not alleviated by vivid fantasies or looking at porn. Rather, the overall cycle that includes fantasies, pornography, and masturbation creates an added layer of emotional and spiritual longing, and an added layer of guilt that the sex addict feels a need to repress, justify, or seek to meet yet again through fantasies, porn, and self-sex. These are "cheap substitutes" with high costs for true intimacy and wholeness.

When sexual affairs are added to the mix, the level of guilt is greatly escalated, and even after an encounter with a prostitute, one-night stand, regular meeting with a mistress, or a "virtual" affair, a man is left with even deeper emotional and spiritual longing, and even more intense unmet needs.

Fantasies tend to become more vivid over time—either through more expansive and explicit porn viewing, or through affairs. The more vivid the fantasy life of a sex addict, the more a sex addict tends to seek out even more titillating imagery. Over time, he needs more exciting and stimulating images in order to achieve the same level of sexual arousal. This is a vicious cycle within the overall vicious cycle of the addiction.

The fantasy, of course, is escalated by the pornography, and pornography stimulates the lust that is expressed in self-sex. Sexual affairs are often the result of overflowing lust that seeks expression in the real world of identifiable individuals. The affairs and self-sex may bring temporary sexual relief, but because neither self-sex nor affairs addresses the deepest needs in the man's life, those needs remain—and grow.

OUR ENEMIES CAN BE DEFEATED AND OVERCOME

How then can we stay in the fight long enough to move from bondage to freedom in our lives? We need to understand where the battleground is. Our flesh produces a certain way of thinking that is attached to our sexual lives. This thinking develops ruts in our brains. Then the ruts in our brains create ruts in our lives. These ruts develop life patterns that become so overwhelming that we need to get everything into the fight in order to overcome.

These ruts in our brains and habits in our minds form our strongholds, and they are the battleground in the fight for freedom and purity. This word "stronghold" is found in Paul's letter to the Corinthians:

> *For the weapons of our warfare are not of the flesh but have divine power to destroy strongholds. We destroy arguments of every lofty opinion raised against the knowledge of God, and take every thought captive to obey Christ* (2 Corinthians 10:4-5, ESV).

As defined here, a stronghold is an argument, or a prideful ("lofty") opinion. It's an idea or a conviction in the mind, such as:

"I am unwanted."

"I am unloved."

"I am unacceptable."

"Sex is my greatest need."

The image in this verse is that my convictions and opinions are something I am arguing over with God, and they are like a dungeon, functioning as a mental hideout, where I escape the truth coming back from God. He tells me that He loves me, but I hunker down and keep on believing that I am unlovable and unacceptable. These strongholds are the result of lies (arguments), anchored deep in my life, and these lies and the places they reside need to be torn down. How do we do that?

We tear down strongholds with weapons of power, weapons from God. It's not a physical fortress, so we don't use physical weapons. This is spiritual work, and we have weapons from God for two major areas.

First, a man needs to understand the truth of his own history—the story of pain, anger and fear, the story of disconnection, sorrow, broken relationships, broken families and the sexual shame in his life. Every man needs the humility to seek a guide to help walk him through his story, to help him see what has contributed to his current state. Then those memories and events need to be grieved, owned and healed, so the pain can diminish. We are destined to misunderstand our stories, but we must understand the impact of our stories on our sexual lives. Acknowledging our histories is the first step in tearing down our strongholds and being renewed by God's Word and His truth about our lives.

This kind of work is filled with divine weapons for tearing down strongholds. For example, we start to tear down strongholds simply by identifying and exposing our stubborn and false thoughts, our lies and wrong convictions. Then a major weapon is the renewing of the mind with God's Word and prayer. In prayer we receive comfort. In prayer we talk to God about our old, hurtful memories; we tell Him how much it hurt; we renounce the lies that were foisted on us that day; we listen to God tell us the truth, and we hide that truth in our hearts. We forgive others, uprooting in prayer our own bitterness and judgments against ourselves.

Second, a man needs to learn new relationship skills in the context of a biblical view of sex and marriage. We have mentioned above the need for men to be mentored in intimacy and healthy sexuality. We must realize that no woman can "fill the holes" in our soul, and they need to be let off the hook for this. Where we have used sex as a tool to feel loved, nurtured and accepted, we need to expose this hurtful way, and get healed of what drives this behavior. We need to forgive ourselves and seek forgiveness where we have harmed others. Learning how to love with a pure heart, and pursue sex as a capstone of authentic intimacy—this is what will tear down strongholds!

Strongholds in our culture have kept our homes and churches from teaching and mentoring us in the biblical view of sex and purity. Men have not been mentored well in the skills of intimacy, honesty, and vulnerability. We have not taught much about the levels of intimacy that precede sexual intimacy, levels that make a relationship meaningful and rewarding. We are living in a fast culture that worships instant gratification, rather than honoring the slow, loving development of intimacy, connection and bonding. Along with intimacy skills, we need to learn healthier conflict-resolution skills. We need to learn how to listen to our spouse, and respond to her needs. God made us for intimacy and bonding, but our culture is neglecting it, and too many of our churches are dead silent about healthy sexuality.

This lack of learning about healthy relationships, healthy sexuality, and godly sex in our marriages is producing an undisciplined, ungodly and destructive way of life for us in the church. The enemy is distracting us with a sexual culture that lures us away in tantalizing fantasy. He distracts us from the work of grace needed to address our struggles with shame and our flesh.

Our shame tries to strip us of our courage to fight. Our flesh becomes "automatic" and keeps us from living in God's resources. We live in our own feeble independence. These enemies keep pastors from shepherding. They keep fathers from leading. They keep young men from fighting.

They keep our young boys dazed and confused. And sexual strongholds grow in the midst of such weakness and confusion.

What can be done to counteract these building blocks for sex addiction?

We turn there next.

QUESTIONS FOR REFLECTION OR DISCUSSION

1. In your journal, be honest with yourself about how many strongholds are a part of your life.

2. Have a discussion with a friend, Bible study group, or support group about these strongholds. You might pay special attention to your history and how they developed in your life.

3. Ask yourself, journal, and discuss the concept of blessing. Did you feel that your father and your mother blessed you by unconditionally loving you and saying they were proud of you.

4. If you are really courageous, think about any experiences of abuse you experienced as a child, adolescent, or teenager. Think of sexual, emotional, or physical types of it. You might want to find a book about types of abuse. Mark's book, *Healing the Wounds of Sexual Addiction* (see the resource section) has a chapter on this, for example.

6

THE HEART OF THE MATTER

Stan was the pastor of a five-hundred-member church, and the people loved him. But Stan had a secret. He had never outgrown the sexual struggle with lust and self-satisfaction, which had been his secret sin while growing up in a Christian home. This internal conflict had left him defeated and despondent in high school, but by the time he went off to college Stan was dealing with his shame more easily.

Campus ministry became a training ground for Stan, and since he was a spiritual leader on the campus, no one was surprised by his announcement that he felt called to go to seminary. His girlfriend of two years, Leanne, became his wife in the summer after graduation, and life seemed great as they made their plans for full-time ministry. Back home, Stan's pastor and family friends were enthusiastically supportive of his plans to be a pastor.

But Stan's problem with lust and self-sex had grown to include occasional pornography use during his college days. He was too proud to ask for help, so he never confessed it to anyone. Besides, he reasoned, it wasn't that big a deal and no one would ever guess, anyway. Stan often prayed for God to take the problem away, but he would never give it up to God for keeps. Leanne never knew or even suspected that Stan had a secret in his life. But four years into his first pastorate, Leanne discovered the pornography on his computer. She was devastated. When she confronted Stan later that evening, he wept. He told her his history, and vowed that, now at last, he will get really serious about quitting. She seemed relieved.

But Stan struggled even more. Even more? Why?

Here's part of the answer: Jesus met a man at the pool of Bethesda one day, and He asked the man if he wanted to get well. But the man went into a defense of his victimhood, which Jesus later called sin. The man was sinning because he was not taking care of himself, but instead was living in dependency on others. There was no strength to his faith. He was waiting in the false hope of an elusive cure, and remaining an invalid, and not just physically. He was emotionally, mentally and spiritually diseased, too.

Stan was like that man. In fact, this describes so many of us when our stubborn sexual struggles keep us so defeated that we are mentally, emotionally, and spiritually weak. We are empty of what it takes to overcome. Enslaved to our impulses and patterns, we are weak in faith. We are weaker in obedience. We would rather keep our sin than get well. This leaves us vulnerable to attack and a liability for others since we are not in prime fighting condition.

After Leanne confronted Stan, he was better for several days. In fact, he felt like he had been delivered, and he began to think that he was healed. Truth is, his shame and humiliation, along with her anger and disappointment, had him shell-shocked so that Stan couldn't even get excited about sex if he wanted to.[36]

No, Stan was not healed. Even the deliverance of Israel from Egypt was a process, not an event. Stan had not committed to a healing process. *While we believe that God can do the miraculous, this is generally not the case*

---

36 This is the false sense of "healing" that has happened to many a man in the immediate aftermath of having been "busted" by the wife. Sadly, it is purely mental and emotional, and has nothing to do with God's deliverance.

in dealing with sexual sin. In fact, about ten days after Leanne confronted him, Stan found himself up late at night working on a sermon. Searching for an article on the Internet, he was suddenly filled with the temptation, again. He stopped. He thought, *Incredible! How in the world, could I have the desire to do that?* But at that moment, even after he had devastated his wife and feared becoming disqualified for ministry, Stan found himself still battling a strong desire to look at porn.

Even after the pain of being humiliated in front of his wife and seeing the hurt in her face, how could it be that Stan still found himself overcome with desire to look at porn. Still? How could he even be thinking of porn? But he was.

At that moment, struggling with the temptation, Stan felt moved by God's Spirit with the same question that Jesus asked: "Do you want to get well?" He was stunned, for deep in his heart he heard his own answer to the question: *No,…I don't. I need it.. I need the feeling that I get from it.* Stan was shocked by this answer that rose up from the inside. Amazingly, he did not want to get well. He was lost in his habit and the comfort of the ruts he lived in. For the first time ever, he realized what a powerful question it was that Jesus was asking.

God is always asking questions to help people see the mess they are in. Three of His questions are perfect for the man struggling to be free.

DO YOU WANT TO GET WELL?

Growing up in a moral Christian home, lust and self-sex had been Stan's secret comfort and companion. First, it brought relief to him as a sexual being, but second, it also was a pleasant diversion when he was sad, mad, glad, or afraid. Vowing to remain sexually pure until marriage, it was how he had survived without sex in college! He was entitled to this release as a reward for sexual obedience while dating. But he wrestled in his heart—his divided heart. Even after having been humiliated in front of his wife, he still had a divided heart.

Most who struggle with sexual strongholds will recognize Stan's honesty. When your heart is divided, Jesus wants to ask you, "Do you really want to be healed?" Like most questions that God asks, they are not asked so that He can learn something, but for us.

In the Sermon on the Mount, Jesus said, "Blessed are the pure in heart, for they shall see God." Purity is the condition to "see" God, and "see" His presence in your life. This is the single, greatest motivation for having a pure heart and being free from sexual bondage: *you will see God.* Instead of seeing sexual images and fantasies, you will "see" His healing presence in your life.

Take note: *The greatest reason to be healed and delivered from your sexual strongholds is so that you can see God in your life. Then others can see Him in your life as well.*

We have worked with many men over the years, and we have found that the men who do *not* want to be free waste a lot of time, energy, and money coming to our offices weekly. But the men who break their stubborn sexual struggles and get free at last, are the men who got honest and push through their denial and defensiveness. They want to see God work in their lives, and they want to learn to live in grace and in truth.

Let's be like that and break through. Let's acknowledge that part of us wants to be free, and part doesn't. The Apostle James describes this condition in his letter when he speaks of a man being "double-minded" (see James 1:8). The word for "mind" is the Greek work used for "soul." We are divided in our souls. Part of our soul wants to submit to God and be free, but another part of our soul wants to keep the bondage of the behavior. But note well what James writes in verse 7: *A double-minded man will never have what he wants!*

Get that? With a divided soul—wanting, but not wanting—a man will never get healed.

Is this your problem?

For many men it is. It's serious. It's defeating. It may be why you are unable to get free.

What can you do about it?

First, you need to *want to* do something about it.

Ask. Seek. Knock. Bang on God's door!

Pray for God to purify your divided heart. Tell Him, "I am willing to have You purify my heart, and take away the desire for my sexual sin. I am willing." (Some of you may need to back up from that and start by declaring to God, "I am willing to be made willing." That is, "God, I am not willing today, but I am open to letting you intervene in my heart anyway that You want, and in the days to come, I am willing for You to help me to become willing.")

When you are willing (and we hope it is today, since you find yourself reading this book), then it is time to get up! Get up and start walking in some new behaviors. These new behaviors might seem risky and scary, but they are absolutely necessary.

Do you want to get well? Get up and find a safe person with whom you can talk.[37] Is there a man who has shared his testimony at a men's gathering at your church? Is there a man you know of who has found his freedom in this area? Find a trustworthy, grace-filled person like a pastor or Christian counselor, and tell them you need help. Ask for their help.

Admitting, confessing, and *talking out* your story are the courageous next steps you must take. Simply talking about your struggle and situation requires great courage and faith, but is often the first bold step you must take when you get up and start walking! You will be surprised that your story will actually cause a "safe" person to love and respect you even more. We know. It happens to us as counselors all the time. People walk into our office, tell their story, and we are filled with compassion and respect for them. Yes, this is what happens in the hearts of the "safe" people.

Do you want to get well?

---

37 By "safe person" we mean someone you can trust with your secrets, someone who keeps secrets, who will still accept you after your secrets come out, and someone who "gets" you. A "safe" person gives grace and accepts you no matter what your story reveals, and is spiritually wise enough to give you truthful feedback. A "safe" person is that person in your life who is most like Jesus to you.

WHAT ARE YOU THIRSTY FOR?

The second question comes from John 4, the gospel story of the woman at the well. She had an obvious thirst for love and acceptance. She thirsted to be wanted, to be chosen, to be honored and esteemed. Her thirst had led her through five marriages and five divorces, and she had become a social outcast. By the time Jesus met her, her failures had left her really empty, lonely, and dry!

The woman came to the well because she needed water, but she needed something greater than stagnant water from Jacob's well. She now had a thirst for forgiveness and new life, and she hoped that worshiping on the right mountain would quench her thirst. She came to the well with deep emptiness and shame that was heartbreaking. She had a soul-thirst.

We, too, have a soul-thirst, and it is at the source for our own sexual longings.

Whoops. Slow down. Did you read that? Read those last two lines again.

Most of our sexual longings are a reflection of a thirst for the same things that woman was thirsty for. Our homes were not perfect, and we grew up with thirsty souls, thirsty for more love and acceptance, approval and affirmation. No matter how old we are, we must understand that we are still empty and thirsty for these things. They don't just go away. These longings can continue to haunt and torture us through our single years and well into our marriages. These longings reveal we have a thirst that has never been quenched.

This is the reason that we often fight in our marriages. If we came to the marriage having not been well loved, accepted, honored, and affirmed in our homes, we expect our spouse to give us this kind of love and respect. But she was waiting to get it from me, while I was waiting to get it from her! Two empty people, two thirsty people, hoping the other person would quench their thirst. Are you getting this? When you are expecting each other to fulfill the deepest longings of your heart that only God can fulfill, it's a setup for a disaster.

The woman at the well had come to view her thirst and longing as only a physical and emotional longing. She did not see that it was a spiritual thirst.

We too often see our sexual longings and fantasies as only physical and emotional longings. We do not see them as a spiritual thirst. Our soul is empty and longing for the Living Water. We are thirsty for love and respect, for honor and acceptance that can satisfy and fill us.

We reach for sex, but we are still thirsty. Still lonely. Still empty.

What's the deal? What is it that we are thirsty for? Most men have never had to think about this question.

Being made in God's image, and being made for Him, our deepest thirst is for intimacy with Him. Let's repeat that: *Your deepest thirst, as His child, is for intimacy with Him.* We are hardwired to connect with God. If we don't pursue intimacy with Him, then we will have a haunting thirst in us. We will never be satisfied. Sometime around puberty we began to link this thirst to sex, and then if we weren't careful, we got trapped! This confusion is spelled out in this mind-blowing quote: "The young man who rings the bell at the brothel is unconsciously looking for God."[38]

Ultimately, the struggle is spiritual and so must be the cure. Remember what Jesus said: "Everyone who drinks of this water [in Jacob's well] will be thirsty again, but whoever drinks of the water that I will give him will never be thirsty again" (John 4:13-14, ESV).

Would you be willing to consider that your sexual problem has a spiritual root? Granted, you are thirsty. There is no doubt that you are thirsty! But you are drinking from the well that can never satisfy your thirst. If you are going to drink from the well that never runs dry, then you must find the answer to this question. "What are you thirsty for?"

ARE YOU WILLING TO DIE TO YOURSELF?

This is our third question. When people came to Jesus telling Him that they wanted to be His disciple, His response was quite blunt.

---

38 Bruce Marshall, *The World, The Flesh, and Father Smith* (New York: Houghton Mifflin, 1945), 108.

However, it is one of the greatest principles for spiritual growth ever delivered: "If anyone wishes to come after me, Let him deny himself and take up his cross, and follow me" (see Matthew 16:24; Mark 8:34; Luke 9:23).

The cross is the symbol of death. When you deny yourself and take up your cross, you are declaring that you are prepared to "die" to anything that is going to keep you from following Jesus Christ. To overcome your sexual struggles it is imperative that you come to see that the way you are thinking, feeling and behaving now will not take you to a newer place of freedom. You cannot find real freedom without a drastic "death" on the inside.

It has been well said that if you always do what you've always done, then you'll always get what you've always got. And right now, you are pretty much doing what you've always done! Your flesh automatically produces more of what you already have, which is automatically familiar to you. Your sexual stronghold is automatically familiar.

Think about it. Did you look at porn this week? Did you look at it last week? Did you look at it the month before? Do you do it every week? Did you do it last year? Did you do it the year before? Is looking at porn on a weekly basis pretty much what you have always done? If so, then you are always doing what you have always done, and you've trained yourself that way! Therefore, if you are going to get free you will have to do something different, something you've never done before.

And that presents the difficulty: coming to the point of consistently doing something different.

To start, you need something from God—It is called brokenness. You need to die to the control of your automatic self, the control your flesh patterns have over you.

To let God heal you, you must be willing to die to yourself and your automatic ways of coping. In brokenness, you are letting go of your own power and experiencing Christ's power. In dying to self you are admitting you are powerless and surrendering control to Christ.

When you get to this point, you have to be honest about the following:

Your pride (*I can do it alone. I don't need Christ*);

Your arrogance (*I'm not that bad*).

Your anger (*It's not fair that my battle is so hard*).

Your shame (*I am a bad person, surely no one will ever love me*).

To die to these thoughts and emotions is to feel them, but move beyond them. To die to yourself is to surrender your own coping strategies to God, and consider them no longer an option for you. This kind of brokenness comes only from God. When you die to your selfish ways of coping, you will find that God is at work, delivering you from yourself.

This is not the same thing as giving up, but rather giving in. Die to your own power and give in to powerlessness, and then begin to learn who God is, the love He has for you and how you can walk in His power. Remember that Jesus *let* Lazarus die, so that the power of God could be demonstrated. You can't rise up to walk in newness of life, until you first die to an old way of living. There can be no resurrection until there is a death.

Are you willing to acknowledge your sexual sins?

Are you willing to see that your automatic coping strategy is to go to some sexual behavior?

Are you willing to die to yourself, and to your sexual ways of coping?

When you are willing, God will meet you in your new stance of emptiness. As you empty yourself of how you medicate yourself, using sex as a comfort, a drink, or a coping strategy, then God will meet you in that emptiness. Die to yourself. Invite God into these places, asking for grace and forgiveness. Die to these by counting them as dead-end ways. Then submit yourself to God to learn new coping skills. Ask Him to raise you up to walk in new ways of life.

You will then be ready to learn how to "let grace set the pace."

A PRAYER FROM THE THREE QUESTIONS

Dear Lord Jesus,

Thank You for providing for my healing, for providing for my thirst, and for providing a new life of freedom. I confess that I have lived away from You and that I have doubted Your power to help me in this area. I confess that I have quenched my thirst with what does not satisfy. I confess that I have been living the Christian life out of my own resources. I present myself to you now, that your grace would strengthen and transform me. (See Hebrews 13:9 and Romans 12:2.) Amen.

QUESTIONS FOR REFLECTION OR DISCUSSION

1. We have provided a basic self-scoring test at the end of the book to help determine if addiction is present. Did you take it? If so, are you willing to get some help if you scored in the addiction range?

2. Share your answers to the three questions or discuss them with someone or your group.

7

THE GAME CHANGER

One word frees us of all the weight and
pain of life: That word is love.

—SOPHOCLES

I have loved you with an everlasting love; therefore
I have continued my faithfulness to you.

—JEREMIAH 31:3, ESV

Larry made his first-ever appointment with a counselor for help. When he entered the room, his face was expressionless, and he had no energy. His marriage wasn't right, he said. He loved his wife, but ignored her. No connection there. They didn't really fight, much. He had never hit her. He wasn't angry. At least, he didn't feel angry. Perhaps he was depressed, but he didn't know why.

He was a couple of years into this, his second marriage, with three energetic, young stepsons, with whom he was slowly learning to relate. But every night Larry would come home and disengage. After dinner he would move to the reclining chair in front of the television, where he would sit all evening. He would sip beer after beer until he sank into a drunken slumber. He was MIA, missing in action in his own home.

In his second counseling session he felt a grieving in his heart. Something had him deeply ashamed, and he could feel it now. He knew what it was, too, and he was finally ready to confess it. Twelve years ago, Larry had cheated on his first wife with a meaningless one-night stand. Long ago. In the past, in his first marriage. He didn't love that woman! It didn't mean anything to him. He didn't know why he had done it.

His shame had put his heart in a prison, locked away from God. He drank himself to sleep every night, and checked out from his needy family for two reasons. First, he could not receive forgiveness from God. Second, because of that, he could not forgive himself. Over the years, Larry had lived in the shame of being unforgiven, a place of spiritual darkness where his mind would not even go to the topic of God's love for him. As far as he figured, his adultery was so shameful—such a mark against him—that there was no point in talking to God about His love and forgiveness.

Our shame always causes us to drop our chins and hide. We feel so unworthy because of what we did (or are doing), that we shrink back spiritually. When the noise of our daily activity fades away, we are left alone in silence with our thoughts, feelings, and regrets.

We go into our caves to hide emotionally. While in there we can decide we are too unworthy to get engaged with our families, or to show up at church on Men's Ministry Night. We decide we are unworthy of the love of God. Virtually every man we have ever met doesn't really believe that God loves him. He can say he believes God loves him, but in his heart, he really doesn't.

WHAT MATTERS MOST

Our earliest Bible lesson as children was that *God is love*, and He loves us. It's kind of strange that we stumble, still, on this first lesson.

The greatest commandment, according to the words of Jesus, is to "love the Lord your God with all your heart and with all your soul and with all your mind" (Matthew 22:35-38). Wouldn't it stand to reason that this must also be our greatest need? God is love, and He created us so that we would deeply desire to give and receive love—and when you learn the depths of His love, it changes everything.

He also made us so hormonal and sensual. The problem on our end is that because of sin, we often feel that our craving for sex, our appetite for sex, is the way we feel loved. Then we succumb to temptation. We fail again, and then feel shameful and despicable. So many of us live in the cycle of shame, where we do pretty well all week long, but then get lost in lust on Friday or Saturday, then rededicate our lives to God on Sunday. Then it happens all again the next week.

Worse, like Larry, our minds are filled with sexual clutter like a dirty garage, and we struggle to believe that God loves us. As men, we are so performance-oriented and so competitive with one another that we wrongly transfer that same model onto God, therefore feeling that God doesn't love us because of our failures. The failure stops us from understanding the depths of God's love for us, and we feel that God is angry with us all of the time.

One man said, "I feel so guilty and terribly ashamed some days. Those days when my sexual past is triggered, memories rise up and haunt me, and on some days, regrettably, I am so tortured with desire that I actually have the crazy thought that I would abandon God and my family just for one day, to taste it all again! I hate this! I wonder how God can love me. I deserve any punishment God would want to give. I'm not worthy of His love and blessings. He accepts me because Christ died for me, but surely He doesn't love me."

In this way, sexual stains can single-handedly make a man feel that God is mad all the time and that He struggles to love someone who has been so trashed. Is it true?

God Is Not Mad at You

The book of Isaiah was written some 700 years before Jesus was born in the manger. In chapter 53 of this book we have this amazing prophecy describing Christ's death for our sins, amazing for its descriptive detail about how Jesus would be crucified, and what it would mean. He was beaten and crushed,...

> *He was pierced through for our transgressions, He was crushed for our iniquities.... Like a lamb that is led to slaughter...My Servant, will justify the many, as He will bear their iniquities.... He Himself bore the sin of many..."* (Isaiah 53:5,7,11,12, NASB).

In this astonishing passage, we have the clear prophetic word from God the Father, hundreds of years in advance, that the Messiah, the Lord Jesus Christ, would take our sins away, and that we would be made right with God. Now let us ask a simple question: What follows this good news of Isaiah 53? That's right, Isaiah 54.

After being told in Isaiah 53 that our sins will be taken away, the first words of Isaiah 54 are, "Shout for joy...break forth into joyful shouting and cry aloud" (Isaiah 54:1, NASB)!

Why shout for joy? Why start singing? What's up? Well, because our sins have been taken away. We are forgiven! We have been made righteous before God.

Then Isaiah moves forward to a verse that we are excited to show you:

> *To me this is like the days of Noah, when I swore that the waters of Noah would never again cover the earth. So now I have sworn not to be angry with you, never to rebuke you again* (Isaiah 54:9).

What's this? Incredible! After He has our sins removed, forgiven, and taken away by Christ, God follows this with the amazing revelation: He will not be angry anymore!

God is no longer mad at us.

Read it for yourself.

Don't misunderstand this. There are consequences for our sins. But so many of us have been taught to believe that God is mad at us for sinning, and that we can never expect a blessing from Him. Another man told us, "I used to get so defeated when from the pulpit my pastor would say things like this, "God won't bless you because of that sin; He will put you on the shelf. I can still hear it in my head today." Can you hear a man say this, "Well, shucks, I looked at porn again last night, so I don't need to be praying and asking God for anything. Not today. Not until I lay down a decent track record of obedience, for a few days in a row."

I know, you've probably heard this because so many teach directly or indirectly that God is disappointed with us, that He's frustrated with us for our disobedience, for our lack of faith, for not reading our Bible, or for not praying enough. And if He's mad about that stuff, imagine how he feels about a man with sexual sin.

We have been poorly trained to believe that God is ready to "get us back" for sinning, and so that's why bad stuff happens in our lives. Our car breaks down, our dishwasher breaks, our children get into trouble, or our business suffers—anything like this happens because He is trying to teach us that He is very disappointed at us for our sexual misconduct. We are silently convinced that our theology is true: I sin so bad, so He is mad.

The truth is, if we all got what we deserved, we would all be in Hell. The ancient pagans believed that they had to change their god's attitude toward them by appeasing him with sacrifices and good works. But this is not how our Heavenly Father operates.

His anger was exhausted at the cross. Both the penalty phase and the punishment phase for our sins are over and finished. Christ paid both. If you are a believer in Jesus Christ, you have received His death for your death and His life for your life. That means that God is finished punishing someone for your sins. He chose the cross of Christ to be the focal point of His wrath, and there, at the cross, He finished being mad. Now He's done.

However, He is not finished transforming your soul and delivering you from your current sin patterns of your flesh. Oh, no. He still wants to walk with you daily in that work. But He is finished with His punishment. He's free to deal graciously with you, and He's no longer mad at you. He loves you. He doesn't *approve* of your sins (and He has a plan to fix that), but He has *accepted* you completely.

Note this well. When you fail and fail again, but you cry out to God for help, that cry in your heart is the work of the Spirit of God. That discontent is not shame. That cry in your heart is the love of God in you, constraining you, and groaning to bring forth new behavior. That is good work! Thank God that He still convicts you of your sin, and plants a longing in your heart for new things. Be on guard when there is no conviction, for it's a sign that your heart has become desensitized and hardened because of your sin. Agree with God about your sin. Confess and turn from it, and His love will cleanse you from it.

Remember, we are forgiven and loved, but He hates the sin. It affects and breaks our relationship with God. He is daily working to deliver us from the ruts of lust. Don't confuse relationship and religion. God is working to deliver us because our relationship has been established by the cross and He is now operating in grace toward us. Religion is about performance and punishment. Relationship is about love and acceptance, and a new kind of performance that emerges by the grace of His love which is at work in us.

In fact, look further into this chapter of Isaiah: "If anyone stirs up strife, *it is not from me*" (see Isaiah 54:15, emphasis added).

Other people will be offended by your secret sins, when they find out about them. They may well stir up strife, but it will not be from the Lord. They may condemn you and terrorize you. But God does not condemn or terrorize you. If (see verse 17) they fashion weapons against you (verbal assaults? slander? accusations? judgments? condemnation? publishing your sin in the church bulletin?), that weapon will not prevail. Such weapons cannot prevail against those who are in Christ Jesus. He is our Righteousness.

God is not mad, even if other people are.

God wants to grow you in righteousness (see verse 14). Most often other people just want to bury you in condemnation.

God is finished judging and condemning your sin. Other people might only be getting started.

I know, this might sound to you like we are speaking a foreign language. But you can read all of the New Testament, and you will not read about God being mad at you for your sins. The unbeliever is still under the wrath of God (see Ephesians 5:6), but not the believer in Christ who has become a child of God.

Think of the father in the prodigal son parable. Do we ever read that the father was angry? Even when he knew that his son had blown the money on prostitutes? When the son came home, did the father "wear him out" with a belt? No, He rejoiced. Rejoiced? Yes, after all of that sinning, the father rejoiced that the young man had come home.

Romans 5:1 confirms this. It says that we have *peace* with God through the Lord Jesus Christ. *Peace.* He's not mad.

Romans 8:1 is another one, and it hits the truth dead on: "There is now no condemnation for those who are in Christ Jesus." *No condemnation!* That sounds as though He's not mad.

Now, for sure, God does have a negative feeling about your sins. The New Testament does give us a glimpse into how God feels about our sins today, on this side of the cross. Paul tells us in Ephesians 4:30, "do not grieve the Holy Spirit." Our sin grieves God. Not because it hurts Him, but because He knows how much it is hurting you. He is grieved that you turned from Him and gave in to lusting and fantasy. He is grieved that you were hurt—maybe bullied, abused, or betrayed—which led you to the Internet for comfort. He is grieved that you have stayed in your sin for so long. He is grieved that it has cost you so much. He is grieved that you have hurt others with your sin. He grieves, but He is not mad at you.

But, you might say, "I keep doing it. I can't quit. Come on, man, I fail over and over, again!"

He loves you, anyway, though He is grieved and He hates the sin. Jesus is ready to forgive seventy times seven. He is not interested in punishing you; your sin is doing a mighty fine job of that, already.

Punishment is not on His mind. Transforming love and kindness is on His mind. Even Paul writes that it is the kindness of God that leads us to repentance, not our fear of His anger (see Romans 2:4).

> **STRATEGY**
> Begin each morning by thanking God for salvation and if you are married, for your wife. Gratitude can get your day started with a positive momentum.

GOD'S LOVE DELIVERS YOU

God wants to deliver us, but His way of delivering us is very different from man's way of deliverance:

- Man's way is to suppress his sexual desires and "white-knuckle" it to overcome temptation.

- Man's way is to "guilt" himself into loving God more, and to berate himself for not loving Him enough—you know, "after all He's done for us!" This kind of theology tends to increase shame, since it is built on performance, and of course, our performance is so bad that our failure always brings more guilt and shame.

- Man's way is to try to "prove" our love for Him by striving to be sexually pure in our own strength, as if we are working for a gold medal. This is not God's way. Our discipline and training in godliness is a work of grace. God works purity *in* us, and then He works it *out* of us. It's by grace, not by works.

God's way is to bless us. He grants us His full and final forgiveness, love and acceptance, which He richly lavishes upon us (see Ephesians 1:7-8). There is no paying Him back for this, otherwise it would not be by His grace (see Romans 11:6). Then He strengthens us with power by the Holy Spirit, Who roots us and grounds us in the love of Christ: as we become more intimately acquainted with this love, the Scripture says we are filled with the fullness of God (see Ephesians 3:14-19). The fullness of God! Now, there's something that could set you free from sexual sin. Let a relationship with your Loving Father drive your sexuality.

"I know. I know," you say. "I've heard it all my life. God loves me. But when will it change my life? How does it free me from sexual sin? How do I 'grasp' it, whatever that means? I know that Scripture says He loves me, but I can't get free from condemnation, shame, and self-pity! How do I sit down on the inside, and rest in the love of God?"

GOD'S LOVE IS SPIRIT-TAUGHT

This transforming love of God, like many truths of our faith, is built on a very certain "knowing."

How do you know that your sins are forgiven? Is it because you heard it in a sermon? Is it because your mother told you? Both may have happened, but is that how you *know* it to be true? No, you know it is true because it came to you by the Holy Spirit. It came from the Lord Himself, on the day that you were born again. The historical fact that He died is in the Bible, but the fact that His death was for your forgiveness, well, isn't that a matter of the Holy Spirit revealing it to you, convincing you? One day you heard it, and you found yourself believing it. It is Spirit-taught.

Ephesians 1:17-18 contains a prayer by the Apostle Paul. He prays that God "may give you the Spirit of wisdom and revelation, so that you may know him better...that the eyes of your heart may be enlightened, in order that you may know the hope to which he has called you."

For the written Word of God to become alive in your heart, God must reveal His word to you, His spirit to your spirit. Spirit to spirit. When the Holy Spirit reveals it to you in your spirit, that is the same thing as having "the eyes of your heart enlightened." Your heart knows it as your spirit "sees" it. The light of the Father shines in your heart and you receive it, believe it, and are immediately persuaded and settled in it.

Now, what is true of the forgiveness of your sins is also true of God's love for you. *It is Spirit-taught truth.* You do not get it any other way. You don't get it because you read in someone's book that God loves you. You don't get it because your pastor told you in a sermon that God loves you. The Holy Spirit is the only one who can persuade you and settle you in the Father's love. It is Spirit-taught. Your pastor can explain it, diagram it, illustrate it, and even do an interpretive dance on stage! But you will never "know" that you know that you know that God loves you until you "see" it with the eyes of your heart. If it happens at all during a sermon or while reading a devotional, it happens because the Holy Spirit orchestrated that moment as a personal teaching moment, opening the eyes of your heart to "see." Unless we know God loves us because the Holy Spirit has taught it to us, we know it only as ink on the pages of the Bible.

After you have failed God again for the thousandth time, how do you know that He's not mad at you, but loves you despite it all? It is because you have been taught this by the Holy Spirit. He has revealed the Father's love to you.

Well, when will He teach it to me? When you are desperate and hungry for it.

How will He teach it to me? When you are on your knees in prayer, with the Bible open in front of you. A great start would be any of the passages on God's love. (Romans 8 would be a good chapter.) When, in prayer, release to Him your condemnation, your shame and self-pity, memory by memory, pain by pain, release it to Him. Let Him fill you with His love and acceptance. With the Word of God open in front of you, and maybe a trusted friend or spiritual mentor by your side, ask the Holy Spirit to teach it to you, and He will open the eyes of your heart, and you will know it.

If you're married, how did you fall in love with your wife? Wasn't it that she gracefully entered the room and you were taken by her beauty? From that moment on, your love for her was the result of *a movement, an influence, in your heart.* She did not convince you that she would be a great date and a good one to marry by going over her resume, a list of her talents, her pedigree, her temperament chart, examples of thank-you notes she has written, and her math and science scores! No. She simply smiled. She laughed. She grinned and winked. She spoke from her heart and revealed herself, and generally carried herself in love and acceptance toward you in such a way that your heart was taken captive, and before long you knew that you knew that you knew that you loved her, too.

It is the same with God the Father, Son, and Holy Spirit in your life. You met them in the Word and in life, and believed the Gospel. They entered your life, and you knew, simply, that you were forgiven and loved. Today, They continue to "reveal" Themselves to you as you meet Them in the Bible. They move in your heart, and you come to see the fullness of your forgiveness, and you rest in Their love and acceptance. The Holy Spirit opens the eyes of your heart to see that you are loved. He influences your heart, and it settles there.

We want this book to help you do the work that will set you free from the sin that so easily besets you. But if you are not convinced that God loves you and forgiveness is a finished, settled matter, then you will struggle to be set free. The love of God (complete with His full and final forgiveness) is the most powerful force in the universe. It has the power to transform a person by diminishing shame and dissolving self-condemnation.

- He loves you.

- He forgives you.

- He no longer holds your sins against you.

- His love and forgiveness can change your heart and set you free from the lust that controls your life.

Get on your knees before the Lord for the next several days and weeks as you read this book. With Romans 8 open before you, ask the Holy Spirit to open the eyes of your heart to see, to know, the truth of God's love for you. You will know when the Holy Spirit teaches you. Then it will begin to change you. This is the love of God that constrains us. It will begin to change the way you think, the way you feel, and the way you act. Your relationship with God and His love will begin to change the way you relate to others.

Here is Romans 8:31-39, amplified for the man who is struggling to know God's love:

If God is for me, who can be against me?

If He gave His own Son for me, will He not also with Him graciously give me purity of heart and victory over my sexual strongholds?

Even if Satan or my sister-in-law bring a charge against me, it is God who has acquitted me. What if someone condemns me? Christ Jesus is the one who cancels that.

Who can separate me from the love of Christ? What if I should fall to sexual temptation because I'm worn out from tribulation, or distress, or persecution, or because I'm hungry, angry, lonely, or tired!

No, in all things I am more than a conqueror through Him who loved me.

For I am sure that neither death nor life, nor angels nor demons, nor things present nor things to come, nor powers, nor height nor depth, nor anything else in all of creation—no temptation, no lust, no pornography, no masturbation, no adultery, no sexual strongholds of any kind, nor my failures in any way will be able to separate me from the love of God in Christ Jesus my Lord.

Amen.

QUESTIONS FOR REFLECTION OR DISCUSSION

1. Have you ever thought that your sexual sin was unforgivable?

2. Do you harbor in your heart one (or more) secret(s) in your life that you thought if you ever told anyone else, they would go running and screaming out of the room?

3. Have you been judgmental of other men's sexual sins?

4. Is there any value in holding on to your shame? What does it help you avoid doing?

8

THE PARADOX OF GRACE:
WHEN WEAKNESS
IS STRENGTH

*The difficulty is to reach the point of recognizing
that all we have done and can do is nothing.*

—C.S. LEWIS

The world's most famous steam locomotive was an engine built in 1923, and bore the name "The Flying Scotsman." The locomotive was notable for being the first train engine to clock a speed of 100 miles per hour. That was amazing speed in that day, and so this steam locomotive shared its name with one of the fastest men on earth, Eric Liddell, the famous Scottish athlete and missionary. Eric Liddell's life was made more widely known to audiences in America through the 1981 movie, *Chariots of Fire,* which won the Academy Award for Best Movie.

Eric had the most unorthodox running style ever seen in an Olympic race. With his head thrown back, his mouth wide open and his arms flailing at his side, he was such a comical sight that serious athletes from other countries would laugh when they first watched this speedster on a race track. One British newspaper stated that he was the ugliest runner to ever win Olympic gold.[39]

The most famous line from the movie was when Eric's sister, Jenny, begged him to give up his athletics to return with the family to their mission work in China. Eric said to her, *"God also made me fast. And when I run, I feel His pleasure."* In real life, Eric never actually said this.[40] The line was put into the script by the screenwriter, but it has been the most favored quote from the movie, perhaps it is because it is not an inaccurate description of the passion of his life. This statement reveals three acknowledgements about the grace of God in Eric's life.

First, Eric ran because he sensed it was his identity. Though a missionary was who he was called to be, running was who he was born to be. He knew his identity as a gifted athlete, and he fulfilled it.

Second, Eric Liddell had been blessed with a God-given power for running. Though he certainly prepared himself for the Olympics, his speed was not the result of exhaustive training nor the achievement of self-effort. It was a power in him, and he expressed it, no matter how unorthodox or ugly it looked.

Third, the statement reveals Eric's strategy for his life. He didn't run out of a sense of obligation and even a fear of failure. Instead, he ran as if Christ Himself were running in him. The movie captured this relationship in his face, for during a race he would start with a fierce determination in his eyes that eventually yielded itself to a smile as he slid the gears into overdrive and headed to the finish line.

---

39 Simon Burnton, "50 stunning Olympic moments No 8: Eric Liddell's 400 metres win, 1924," *The Guardian,* January 4, 2012). (http://www.theguardian.com/sport/2012/jan/04/50-stunning-olympic-moments-eric-liddell) (Accessed December 31, 2014).

40 As noted in "Quotations," website of the Eric Liddell Centre, Edinborough, Scotland (http://www.ericliddell.org/ericliddell/quotations) (Accessed December 31, 2014).

Eric Liddell illustrates the grace of God for our lives. The same grace that enabled Eric Liddell to run his way to the Olympic gold helps us to overcome. The three gifts of grace are the same: (1) the *identity*, (2) the *power*, and (3) the *strategy* of grace.

First, grace has granted us a new identity. *"Christ, who is your life."* That's a direct quote from Colossians 3:4. When we came to Christ, we came to a cross, and the cross means death. We came to our death when we came to Christ, so that He could live in us. His life, in place of ours, is our new identity. Galatians 2:20 says "I have been crucified with Christ and I no longer live, but Christ lives in me. The life I now live in the body, I live by faith in the Son of God, who loved me and gave himself for me." Galatians 3:29 describes us as co-heirs and in John 15:15 we are called Jesus' friends. This is who you are.

Second, if you think you are going to fiercely strong-arm your lust problem away, it will not happen. We do not fight by doubling down or buckling down. Although we make a firm decision to deal with our sin, willpower alone is like shadowboxing. We are saved by grace through faith, and we will win the fight of our lives the same way, by grace through faith. Grace is a power. The power for sexual purity comes by grace.

Third, the law exposes but grace delivers. The law doesn't help me with my sin. Rather, it exposes my sin. The law does not make me stronger. Grace delivers me with a new strategy: Grace trains me where the law fails to change me. Grace applied is the true New Testament strategy that actually trains me to live in power gained through purity.

GRACE GRANTS US A NEW IDENTITY

God knew that in our own strength we would never be able to live the Christian life in all of its holiness and purity. He challenges us to do so, but, He knew we couldn't do it, so He devised a plan to help us.

His plan was that when Christ died on the cross, God would place us in Christ, and then we, as sinners, could die there, too. Then, when He raised Christ from the dead, He would raise us up to walk in a new life, too. That's just what we read in Paul's letter to the Romans:

We were therefore buried with him through baptism into death in order that, just as Christ was raised from the dead through the glory of the Father, we too may live a new life. For if we have been united with him in a death like his, we shall certainly be united with Him in a resurrection like his. For we know that our old self was crucified with him so that...we should no longer be slaves to sin" (Romans 6:4-6).

The battle plan in the war for sexual purity can be turned on its head right here!

The battle changes when we realize we have a new identity. And because this new identity is that of Jesus Christ, the power that raised Him from the dead is now at work in you. Romans 8:11 says: "If the Spirit of him who raised Jesus from the dead is living in you, he who raised Christ from the dead will also give life to your mortal bodies because of his Spirit who lives in you."

Paul has one name for all of the people who read his letters: saints. He calls us "saints." The word in the Greek for "saint" is the word "holy." It is plural, too, so it is literally translated, *"holy ones."* We are saints, and we are holy people because of our relationship with Jesus Christ. When God now sees us, He sees Jesus Christ. We are indwelt by the Spirit of life in Christ Jesus (see Romans 8:2). And we are now "set apart for God and His service." His life is holy, and His life is now our life in our spirit. By His life in us, we are able to overcome the gravitational pull of sin and temptation. We don't walk alone or under our own power. As we practice His presence and look to His direction, we can walk in victory.

Embrace your relationship with Christ. Stop trying to work a religious activity to get free. Instead, embrace the grace of experiencing Christ as your life. His power will be your power. He is more than near: "But he who is joined to the Lord becomes one spirit with him" (1 Corinthians 6:17, ESV).

The One who created sex in the first place, He who is pure in heart—He is your life! Get up and walk in Him; walk in His life: "As you received Christ Jesus the Lord, so walk in him" (Colossians 2:6, ESV).

The next time you go to shame mode, remember,. God doesn't shame you. The next time you are confronted with a lustful memory, or you break down and look again at porn—He is still with you! He is present to you! In fact, He is present in you! He's still claiming you. He is present to transform you. When you fail, Christ Jesus continues to extend the presence of His life in you. He is in the fight of your life! He is fighting in you, with you, through you, even *for* you! Christ is your new life. He is one with you in spirit. This is the grace of a new identity.

GRACE GRANTS US A NEW POWER

Most of us know grace as "unmerited favor," getting a free gift that you did not deserve.

Grace also begins the transforming power of God. Grace works a work in your heart to deliver you from yourself. How else would you come to faith in Jesus Christ, except that grace created faith in your heart? At the cross, God's grace delivered you from the penalty of sin, but in the rest of your life on planet Earth, God's grace is delivering you from yourself. *Grace is the powerful influence of God that invisibly and mysteriously brings about a change in your heart and mind, which results in a change in the course of your life.*

Under the law of Moses, there was no power like grace. The law told the nation of Israel almost everything they needed to know about how to live for God. It even told them how to behave sexually, and which sexual behaviors were forbidden. But there was no power, no enablement for this obedience. There was no supernatural stamina to help them obey. The law told them what to do, and they had to be committed to do it.

In the New Testament it is different. There is one phrase that never appears in the New Testament: "make a commitment." That's right. We are never scolded and told to be more committed! Do you know why?

Because our power (also called "the flesh") is inadequate.

We have grace instead, the most powerful force in the universe. Take a minute to soberly read this passage out loud:

For the grace of God has appeared...training us to renounce ungodliness and worldly passions, and to live self-controlled, upright, and godly lives (Titus 2:11-12).

Grace does what? Grace trains us. It trains us to renounce our ungodly sexual sins and our worldly passions. It trains us to be self-controlled, which is a fruit of the Spirit. Grace does this. Grace is the power for transformation.

The Greek word in that verse for "training" is a word used for the training of children. This training is a process and often involves discipline and correction. It is part of how maturity develops through growth. Paul is not referring to a lecture series. He is not referring to a sermon. He's not talking about talking! He's writing about a different kind of training, an internal training by the power of God. The point is this: We learn how to get out of our sexual challenges and into a life of purity not by our own strong works for God, but through His strong work in us.

Grace will train a humble, receptive heart—never a self-confident heart. Grace meets us in repentance and trains us. When I fail during this process, I'm in a good place to learn something. I learn that I fail when I am trusting myself. That is it. His life and power make me strong. When I am weak, then I am strong, for the grace of the Lord Jesus Christ mentors and trains me to renounce my ungodly passions and ungodly sexual patterns, and mentors me in trusting the power of His life.

GRACE GRANTS US A NEW STRATEGY

In the battle with sexual longings and fantasies, and even with pornographic visions and vain imaginations, in the struggle over lust, we need the truth about overcoming. Here's the truth: *Keeping the law won't work.* Even if you could do it, it would count for nothing, for Jesus said, "Apart from Me you can do nothing" (John 15:5).

If you try to use a law to overcome sin, you will discover that your sin will grow as if it's on steroids! In fact, the power of sin comes from the law. If you use a law to try to defeat sin, just the opposite will happen. The Apostle Paul says in Romans 7:13 that it will make your sin "utterly sinful," immeasurable! In the attempts to get free from sexual sin, the law only makes sin more powerful.

We need to ask ourselves, "If following the law could work, then why would God have put Christ's life in us?" The law was never designed to deliver us from sin in the first place. The purpose of the law is to merely expose to me that my sin is killing me, that I need a Savior to deliver me. Therefore, the new strategy is not, "Be stronger!" That is a thorough misconception of the Christian life. Our new strategy from Christ and the Apostle Paul is, "Be weaker." If you are strong, then what is Christ supposed to do? If you are strong and working on getting stronger, then what do you need Christ for?

If you are frustrated and disappointed with yourself, then, sadly, that means that you were trusting in yourself. You were trusting in your own strength to get up and be good for Jesus' sake! That may be religion, but it is not Christianity. And it doesn't work.

We can fulfill the commands of the Father, but we do it now by the power of His life, by the power of the Holy Spirit. Therefore, do not try to follow a law to be more pure for God in your own strength, as a good Christian man. Doing that is a setup for failure!

Do you want to be stronger? Then set your mind on being weaker.

Weakness is the strategy of grace.

Jesus Christ does not have a struggle with sexual sin. Of course not. Jesus Christ, the Righteous One, knew no sin (see 2 Corinthians 5:21). He is sexually pure.

Where does He live now?

He now lives in you, if you have received Him and believed in Him as Savior. Present your body to Him as a living sacrifice (see Romans 12:2). Present yourself to Him, the sexually pure One. Submit yourself to Him (see James 4:7). You can do all things through Christ who strengthens you (see Philippians 4:13).

Tell Him you are in a battle, and that you trust Him to live His life in you. Yield to His life in you, and let His life be reflected *as your life*. That's growing by grace.

Grace has good news for you: No matter what you have done, the Lord Jesus Christ is still living in you. It doesn't matter where you've been, how far you've fallen, how bad it's gotten. With grace, it's about who He is and what He's done, and the power of His life that is working within you. He works in the pain and beauty, for He is after your heart, not perfect behavior. Give Him the gift He wants. Give Him your heart. Come to the end of yourself, and say yes to the grace of God.

CONCLUSION

Trying harder on your own is not going to work. Strength comes in your relationship with Christ. As you give yourself to counseling, to a small group, to accountability with other men, to confessing and renouncing, to exploring your journey, to examining your hurtful attitudes, and to Bible study and prayer, your life will find strength because of the *power of God working upon your heart.* The grace of God is transforming you at your deepest level, the level of identity, and it is bringing about a change in your heart and a change in your behavior.

C.S. Lewis wrote:

> Again, in a sense, you may say that no temptation is ever overcome until we stop trying to overcome it—throw up the sponge.… If you have really handed yourself over to Him, it must follow that you are trying to obey Him. But trying in a new way, a less worried way.… Not hoping to get to Heaven as a reward for your actions, but inevitably wanting to act in a certain way because a first faint gleam of Heaven is already inside you.

"Throw up the sponge" has the same meaning as the American phrase "throw in the towel." It means to give in, to quit. That means we give up trying to attain our sexual purity through works, and we trust in God's grace. We trust in Jesus Christ, and His life *in* us, *through* us, and *for* us. We trust in His life alone. If you've exhausted yourself in the ring, and have worn out your arms swinging in an effort to defeat this opponent, we invite you to throw in the towel. Take off your gloves and give yourself up to grace, which is inside you. It is Christ in you, the hope of glory.

QUESTIONS FOR REFLECTION OR DISCUSSION

1. Have you ever experienced giving up on something only to find that a solution came to you or that someone came along and offered to help? Have you ever simply let go and just asked for help? And suddenly, you somehow found it?

2. Other than sexual sin, have there been other areas of your life that felt unmanageable, that you couldn't do what you wanted to do or stop what you wanted to stop?

3. What is one technique or step you have always tried to use but has never worked to stop your sexual sin? Is it like a law for you? What is one step you could take to replace this "law" with grace?

9

WHAT GOOD IS GOD? (DO YOU WANT TO BE HEALED?)

I am convinced Satan wants to rob me of only one thing,
and that is my faith. He wants to destroy my faith
and make me believe God has forsaken this earth.
—DAVID WILKERSON

Being confident of this, that he who began
a good work in you will carry it on to
completion until the day of Christ Jesus.
—PHILIPPIANS 1:6

I (Mark) got a call from a man who had his own Christian counseling ministry and radio program. He wanted to interview me for his show. As we talked beforehand, he told me his story. It is such a common story, familiar to most of us who have suffered the self-destruction of a sexual compulsion that knows no limits. His involvement started in adolescence with the regular usage of pornography, and it ballooned out of control by the time he was 20. His compulsion became an addiction, and it cost him, not just one, but two marriages. Broken and bruised by the rupture of two divorces, he said, "I woke up one day in my early 30s, feeling empty and alone." He said, "What good is God, what good is living. I was seriously considering suicide."

His life had been built around Satan's lies about how fulfillment and satisfaction could be provided by sex. Now, in the ruin of his relationships, Satan's new lies came in the darkness of suicidal thoughts, and this man gave up. Life had no meaning, no purpose. "If only there were a God who could save me," he thought. Then he said it out loud, "I would be delivered if God were real." In that moment, he had an encounter with the Holy Spirit, one of those mysterious, spiritual moments, when the Holy Spirit opens the eyes of one's heart to see the Father's love. The revelation of love was followed by the clear and distinct notion that God wanted him to rise up and walk with Him into sobriety,[41] into the freedom of living free from the control of sex. "The Father wanted me to get up and participate *with Him* in the cleansing of my life," he said. From that moment, this man began to walk into his freedom. *With Him.* At the time of our phone conversation, he had lived ten years of freedom, and was married again to a supportive, loving wife. He walked. God worked. He walked out what God was working in him (see Philippians 2:12-13).

Now, let's be honest. Though this man had experienced a miracle moment, he still had a journey to walk. As most of us can testify, rare is the story of an instant deliverance from a stronghold, any stronghold. Yet, the miracle is still there for all of us. Though our temptations and struggles are different, the miracle of deliverance is the same. Our miracle is found in the journey of meeting God daily in the battle. The miracle is grace. It's the divine influence upon our hearts that leads to a transformed way of living, as we yield our lives to Him.

---

41 This is a term borrowed from alcoholism. To be sexually sober is to be living under the control and power of the Holy Spirit, experiencing abstinence from habitual, sexual sins, enjoying the freedom of obedience and the freedom from the control of lust and pornography.

The journey is rarely smooth. No, the journey is fraught with a wavy line of inconsistency. For this piece of our lives is so stubborn, and the triggers are strong—and they keep coming! Challenges keep coming. We can pray at home and feel strong and free, only to leave the house for the mall or the grocery store, and get bombarded with visual stimuli. We can watch the game of the week with our friends in innocent fellowship, but then a commercial comes on the screen, and it advertises a sexual plot "tonight at 9:00," and in our minds we leave the room for a few moments to think about what is on our schedule for later that night.

The draw of sex is so overwhelming that even the best of intentions get undermined within the routines of life. Then the shame can come like a double portion after we have drawn a line, only to fall again on the wrong side of that line.

Sexual sins have such a power to condemn us and stir up our shame. Ask most men and they will say, "I can eat too much, drink too much, cuss some, or fuss at my kids, and I repent and move on. But when I look at a woman, I hate where my mind goes; when I think of another woman while having sex with my wife, when I am not available to my wife because I "took care of myself" earlier, when I look at pornography for the third time this week, or this month, or this semester, *I hate it!* I'm filled with anger at myself. I feel my emptiness. I feel my loneliness. I hate who I am. I tell myself I'm such a disappointment to God. I can't be strong. I can't quit. I can't do what's right."

Failure can be so devastating, that it can leave us wondering if God really loves us. It can convince a born-again man to doubt whether he really knows the Lord at all. It can create such shame and despair that a believing Christian will want to give up and quit. Many a Christian man has contemplated suicide in the face of his inability to find freedom.

Don't let failure drive you there. Remember, when your heart cries out after failing again, that this conviction, this crying for change, is the groan of the Holy Spirit in your heart. Though you feel the weight of brokenness at times, don't despair. Don't quit. Don't fall into denial and apathy. And don't lose sight of the goal: sobriety and freedom. God still matters. He is still at work in your life. Thank Him for that!

Richard (from chapter 7) went on to Bible college right out of high school. He was still wearing his invisible nametag: "Unworthy." By the time he turned 14, Richard had discovered masturbation, and it had become a daily routine. After four straight years of this behavior, it was doing its damage to his identity. As a Christian, Richard was convinced that it was a sin for him, mainly because of the lust-filled imaginations of his mind. He prayed and prayed that God would take it away, but it never went away. When he started Bible college, he thought, "Now, I must quit. I can't be with all of these other godly people and continue my secret behavior." But by the second day, Richard got alone and broke his vow. He continued all through college. Frustrated, angry, hopeless, ashamed, he would stare out the window of his dorm room, standing in oppressive darkness, and wonder what God was going to do with him. If God was there to help, then why didn't He?

Then Richard read Psalm 51, and saw that he shared the same battle with King David. He realized that the issue was one of relationship. God is the deliverer. God is the one who cleanses the heart and restores a pure spirit. He does it in the wonder of intimacy. Our relationship with God is never broken because of our sexual sin. Our sin breaks us. We are broken by the shame and despair we fall into. Healing and restoration come through intimacy with the Father. When I repent, when I turn back to Him, I encounter His loving kindness. His love is everlasting. My relationship waits for nothing from Him. I am the one who turned away.

David had turned away in a subtle progression that caused him to end up in the naked arms of Bathsheba. He removed himself from the war front, where he should have been, and opened his heart to the boredom that set in. Then he leisurely went out on the rooftop at dusk. He knew what he was doing. It seemed so innocent, yet it was very intentional. He let down his defense, and stepped out into a different kind of battle. He set himself up by gazing out, like a peeping Tom, a voyeur, to see who might be taking a bath. Bathsheba was no surprise. His heart began to race (adrenaline!) as he turned his heart away. That's why his Psalm _ _ is about restoring our heart to the love of the Father, restoring our heart to the beauty of intimacy.

Richard saw the trap he was in. Like a dog returning to its vomit, Richard was returning to the place where his brain had been wired. In his idle moments, he had trained his brain to go to lust. Without changing this, he was allowing the "training" to continue. He never preempted it. He never fought through the temptations. It wasn't that God was not willing. Richard never fought. He never walked in the ways of submission, presenting himself to God to practice the new behaviors that would rewire his brain and renew his mind.

Where is God? Why doesn't He fix me? As good Christian men we cry out to God for deliverance. We cry out for Him to forgive us, and to remove this craving and chaos. But He never seems to show up.

Where is His help? God seems so mysterious and elusive. It's like He's not doing anything to help us. What gives? What's He doing? *What good is God*, we wonder. *What good is God?*

But God is there. It is we who are not showing up. Perhaps He's asking where we are!

In John 5 we begin to discover why God appears so elusive, and why it only appears He is not helping us. Jesus and his disciples went into Jerusalem, and came walking by a pool of water called the Pool of Bethesda. There was a religious superstition that an angel would occasionally stir the waters with its wing, and the first person to step into the water would be healed. The whole context of this story gives the impression that Jesus did not believe in this particular tradition.

Verse 5 tells us that a man had been there for 38 years waiting to get healed! The Greek word used to describe this man's sickness is the same word that is also used to describe a person as merely weak, feeble, or lacking strength. Though it is a word that can identify a disease, it is also a word that can describe the mere physical fatigue that might remain after a sickness, leaving a person physically feeble and powerless. Interestingly, today this same Greek word is found in the name of a disorder of the body where muscles become fatigued and weak, and in some cases paralyzed.[42]

Apparently this man did not have a physical disease, but he was suffering with some kind of internal, emotional weakness and powerlessness. Here's how we know. After the healing of this man (see verse 14), Jesus tells the man that he has been sinning, and to stop. What was his sin? Apparently, it was taking such a posture of dependency and victimhood that he had grown weak and feeble.

This is just like what happens to us with the sin of our stubborn sexual strongholds. We get so defeated that we become emotionally and spiritually bankrupt. We spend so many years enslaved to our impulses and compulsions, that we grow weak in faith. We then become emotionally, mentally and spiritually weak. We become so weak that we cannot *not* do our secret sin.

Jesus asks this man, "Do you want to get well?" At first glance, this question seems ludicrous. Of course, this man wants to get well. But as C.S. Lewis points out, "Before we can be cured we must want to be cured. Those who really wish for help will get it; but for many people even the wish is difficult. It is easy to think that we want something when we do not really want it."[43]

Jesus asked the man, "Do you want to get well?" After some whining on the man's part about not being fast enough to get into the water, he also complained that he had no one to help him. This reflects his double-mindedness. He wanted to get healed, yet there also was a part of him that had never known anything else but the brokenness. Was Jesus really asking this? "Are you willing to give up the mind-set, and give up the life of weakness and dependency? Is your sin, or the pleasure of it, something that you are willing to live without? Are you ready to stand up in spiritual maturity?"

---

42 Myasthenia gravis (from Greek μύς "muscle," ἀσθένεια "weakness") an autoimmune neuromuscular disease leading to fluctuating muscle weakness and fatigue.

43 C.S. Lewis, *Mere Christianity* (New York: Macmillan, 1960), 99.

Regardless, Jesus said to him, "Arise, take up your pallet, and walk." The man got up. He was healed! What did Jesus do to heal him? Jesus simply told the man "Get up. Start walking." Jesus did not lay his hands on him. He didn't pray over the man. Jesus didn't heal this man so much physically, as He healed him emotionally and spiritually. He healed the man's paralyzed will to walk in faith. The man then joined himself to the healing by getting up, and by walking.

Maybe we see something in this story for us. Give up. Get up. Give yourself to walking.

Give up! Because you have no strength in yourself, anyway.

Get up! Because only you can present yourself to God. You determine whether you will be filled with the Spirit; you determine whether you will be strengthened by His grace. Get up! Present yourself to the Spirit, and do it multiple times a day if necessary. Do whatever it takes.

Start walking! Because Jesus is living in you with resurrection power!

The life of freedom you want to walk in is a life you have never lived before. Read that again. The life you have been living is one of failure. The life you want to live is the life you have never lived! So, your past can still teach you, but only what you can learn from your failures and missteps. Most of the time, you learn to live the life of freedom by walking into it, practicing it, doing it every day, doing it again tomorrow, living it over and over and over—rewiring your brain with new ways of believing, renewing your mind.

We learn from the future as it emerges in our hearts, minds, and wills, with each step of obedience we take. This is why Paul tells us:

> *Since, then, you have been raised with Christ [resurrection power], set your hearts on things above, where Christ is, seated at the right hand of God. Set your minds on things above, not on earthly things* (Colossians 3:1-2).

Learn from your past to figure out what is going wrong and what needs God's attention. Then learn from the future: Set your mind on the life that Christ possesses, the resurrection power that raised Him to the

Father's right hand. According to Ephesians 2:6, we sit there, too! We sit with Christ, in Him, in the heavenly place, at the Father's right hand. Our life is there. With our eyes on Christ, His life emerges underneath our steps of obedience, as we experience Christ's life in us.

Surrender. Give up! When you feel like your next step is your last step, because your compulsion has become unmanageable, then give up. There's nothing in you that can win this battle except resurrection life alone. If you have been disappointed with yourself, that must mean that you were trusting in yourself. Cancel that.

Get up and give Him your faith. Your failure by now has cancelled out your illusions about your own strength in the matter. The battle is a battle of faith, faith in Christ Himself, to live in you and through you the life of purity.

Then walk. Walk in His life, which is in you.

Now you are in the battle. Now God will show you how He delivers.

In the sports world, there is something that athletes do for success. They practice. They practice the same muscle movement over and over and over again. They practice that swing, that throw, that shot, that pitch, over and over until it becomes their new natural. The idea behind this is to so train the muscles that the behavior becomes automatic. This is what the Apostle Paul tells us to do in First Corinthians 9:24-27 (NASB):

> *Run in such a way that you may win. Everyone who competes in the games exercises self-control in all things [they control their muscles to do it, again and again, automatically]. ...Run in such a way, as not without aim; I box in such a way, as not beating the air; but I discipline my body and make it my slave, so that, after I have preached to others, I myself will not be disqualified.*

You walk. He works. This is the battle. This is how it is won.

You walk in the steps of purity. He works His purity into your soul.

You walk in purity every day. You train yourself for godliness every day. Every day. Until it becomes automatic! Give yourself to it every day, as King David gave himself to God's word every day. "I meditate on it all day long" (Psalm 119:97). You exercise these new muscles every day until you rewire your brain, until you are believing new truths, until old habits lose their grip on you, until new habits are formed and become automatic. Remember this thought: "It's amazing how much work it takes to become an overnight success!"

Give up!

Get up!

Start walking!

But walk where? Where do I go? Where do I show up? What do I do in this walk of faith? Give me my next step!

NEW SPIRITUAL MUSCLES FOR BREAKING SIN'S DOMINION

In the Twelve Step program the first three steps match "Give up! Get up! Start walking!" The walk is a walk of grace. It's about showing up and presenting yourself to walk daily with God. When you admit that you have no more personal strength, that you are powerless and your life is out of control, then in the second step you "come to." You come to God: the Father, Son, and the Holy Spirit. You come to believe that God is the only one who can restore your sanity. You come to present yourself to the work of grace in your heart:

> For this is the will of God, your sanctification: that you abstain from sexual immorality; that each one of you know how to control his own body in holiness and honor, not in the passion of lust like [those] who do not know God (1 Thessalonians 4:3-5, ESV).

Here is the passage that tells us exactly what the will of God is for our lives. It applies to all of us. It is His will that we please Him with the way we control our own body in the sexual realm. If you don't know the Father, then you will struggle. Sexual purity is bound up in the intimacy of knowing God as your Father.

Be filled with the Spirit of God (see Ephesians 5:18). Every day. Yield to His control throughout the day. Get acquainted with the Holy Spirit as your constant companion throughout the day.

Let the Word of Christ fill your mind (see Colossians 3:16). Read God's Word. Study sexual purity in the Bible, and let those Scripture verses shape your thinking. Know Christ's mind on sexual topics. Let's His words control your sexual thinking daily.

Put on the full armor of God (see Ephesians 6:11-17), which is essentially your identity in Christ. Put on the belt of truth, which is Christ's life of integrity. Since Christ is the truth (see John 14:6), and He is your life (see Colossians 3:4), then by nature you are a "truth-er" (see Ephesians 4:15). Live in healthy self-awareness (the truth) of your surroundings. Are there triggers on the horizon? Is the grocery store going to be a temptation? Is your secretary too alluring? Is your co-worker a provocative or a temptation? Is the family trip to the beach going to be a struggle? *Then that's the truth!* Don't deny the truth. Be aware of what is happening in your heart, your mind, and your surroundings that can trigger sexual arousal. Be on guard. Stay in the battle, and don't go up on the rooftop. Don't be deceived.

Put on the breastplate of righteousness, which is Christ's righteous life. Believe every day that you are alive with His righteous life. Rely upon His life as your worthiness and reason for acceptance by the Father. When others talk of sexual immorality in the locker room, in the dorm room, in the warehouse, behind closed doors, give no advantage to Satan. Let righteousness control your thoughts, and speak this, "I will not be tempted by that (sexual image), for that is not who I am. I know who I am; *I am the righteousness of God in Christ* (see 2 Corinthians 5:21). *I'm walking in power because I'm walking in purity!*"

Put on Christ who is our peace (see Ephesians 2:14) with God, and let His redemption and forgiveness (see Ephesians 1:7) help you to apply this same peace to all of your relationships, including dating relationships or your committed marriage relationship. Bring the peace of sexual purity into all of your relationships. That girl you are dating is the bride of Christ. That woman you are married to is still the bride of Christ. Be careful how you treat His daughter!

Take up the shield of faith and hide yourself in His truth. Hide your mind from the flaming missiles that fly at us continually from our sex-saturated culture. Believe what God says about love, romance, sex, and marriage, and learn to see these with God's eyes. Let your faith stand against the missiles (triggers) of lust, doubt, shame, and other deceptions of the enemy. Believe that you can live with personal control, that you can live without porn, that Christ living in you can empower you to live without the lust of the flesh. Believe it and live it! Let a life of faith and purity trigger new endorphins in your brain that will excite you about this life with God.

Put on the helmet of salvation. Let it be settled that you are securely and sufficiently forgiven for all sins, and accepted forever. Know that you are His, and that you belong to Him. Pray for God to so protect your mind today that it is free from remembering the former sexual sins that once enslaved you. Let this helmet protect you from the lies of the enemy that can stir up shame and false guilt, that stir up an identity based on shame.

Take up the sword of the Spirit, which is the Word of God, and let the Holy Spirit rewire your brain by training you in speaking Scriptures that set your mind on Christ and your identity in Him. Let His Word divert your mind away from the temptations, triggers, and visions that are the typical schemes of Satan against you daily. Satan will beat you up with despair and discouragement. Stand against him with the specific parts of the Word of God that the Holy Spirit has spoken to you. Use those words as your weapon against a defeated mind-set.

This is how you are trained in godliness. This is the spiritual life.

Stay in this walk of grace. Stay until grace develops new muscles in you.

Old habits will break. Their power will diminish. Miracles will happen.

STRATEGY
If your wife or family has plans that will leave you home alone for an evening or weekend, and you know that is a trigger, make plans with some friends to get out of the house and do something active. Set yourself up for success.

After you give up and get up, you can *start walking* in the steps of sexual purity, training yourself in the holiness of your sexuality, being filled with the Father's love, guided by the Son's Word, and encouraged by the companionship of the Holy Spirit.

What good is God? We hope you know now. His miracles still happen. They come in the *walking out* of what He is *working in* you. God's heart is still leaning toward you. He loves you with an everlasting love. He is working to win your heart. After moments of great struggle and defeat, He arrives with a heaviness in conviction, but He is simply reminding you that He called you to a deeper life, to a deeper walk of sexual purity. He wants you free. Get everything into the fight.

You will love being free!

QUESTIONS FOR REFLECTION OR DISCUSSION

1. Can you create a plan for where you will "show up" this week? For example, (a) at your pastor's office, (b) at a counselor's office, (c) at a support group, (d) at coffee with a friend.

2. Showing up also means showing up emotionally and spiritually. Is there someone in your life this week, like a spouse or a friend, with whom you need to show up and get honest about this area?

3. Would you be willing to "get up" in the morning to start a new spiritual discipline?

10

CAN YOU HANDLE THE TRUTH?

For when Solomon was old his wives turned
away his heart after other gods, and his heart
was not wholly true to the Lord his God.

—1 KINGS 11:4, ESV

Gary pulled into the convenience store parking lot to fill his car with gas. As normal, he checked out the lanes to see which one would give him the fastest exit once he was done. But wait. *Wow. Who is she?* His eyes were drawn to a shapely figure standing next to her car. *Yesss! the gas pump right behind her is open. Sweet.*

Gary pulled up, taking a long delicious look at this gal. Gary had long ago learned the art of acting like he was looking elsewhere with his head turned slightly, but behind his sunglasses he was drawing in every contour of her body.

He opened up his car door and got out, but he did not look at the woman. Image management. In his vanity, he wanted to present himself, like the raising of a curtain on opening night.

Gary swiped his credit card. *I wonder if she's looking this way?* He played it nonchalant. In his narcissistic moment on stage, Gary assumed that this long-legged beauty was looking at him, and he wanted to appear as cool and masculine as possible. Casually, Gary turned his head toward her. She looked over and smiled at him.

Gary smiled back and nodded his head, playing it cool on the outside. On the inside he gasped. *Oh my gosh, she just smiled at me! Wow, her face was electric! Did you see her eyes! I can't believe it. I told you I look good in this white starched shirt. I wonder if she's married. She can't be. Is she single? She's gotta be.*

As the young woman pulled the nozzle from the tank, she changed hands with it and dropped her keys. She set the nozzle in its place and wiped her hands on each other. Then, with her back to Gary, she bent over and picked up her keys.

Gary's eyes were having a feast. *Oh my gosh! Did you see that,...oh, wow ....*

As she rose up the young woman suddenly was aware of what she had just done. *Oh, no, he wasn't watching was he?* she wondered. She glanced back at him, and unfortunately he was looking at her. Embarrassed to death, she smiled awkwardly and got in her car. In a moment, she was turning out of the gas lane, ready to get away.

Something completely different was happening in Gary's mind. *Oh my gosh, did you see that? She smiled at me.* Gary couldn't believe it. He loved it.

Filled with the vain imagination that this young woman was flirting with him, Gary jumped in his car and followed her out of the parking lot. All the while he was behind her, changing lanes when she did, and turning when she did, Gary was being carried away with the thought that a new affair was starting up. He was excited. He fantasized of places and times for a rendezvous in the days to come. His heart was racing. He could feel it. At a red light he saw her look at him through her rear-view mirror. *I knew it. I knew it. She's checking to see if that's me behind her. She's trying to connect. She wants this.* There was a strange connection with the young woman, and Gary felt it in his heart. She was leading him. He was following.

Suddenly she whipped into a parking lot, and Gary pulled in to the next available space a short distance away. His mind was so occupied with images that he did not notice where they were. She was out of her car fast, so Gary parked and jumped out of his. His mind was so lost in fantasy that he didn't realize the woman had pulled into a neighborhood police annex! "That man is following me," she screamed in a voice that rattled Gary out of his drama. Three cops were standing in the front of the building. Gary froze. Two officers approached him. A brief exchange took place between the officers and the young woman, and back again with Gary. Thankfully, she did not want to press charges. She just wanted Gary to leave. One of the officers spoke to him, "You have come close to getting into some serious trouble here, sir. I would advise that you get in your car, go on to work, and you think long and hard about what you've just done."

Gary was embarrassed, humiliated, scared out of his wits. He got back in his car, backed up and drove off at a respectable speed. He couldn't wait to turn the nearest corner and get out of sight. He noticed that his hands and arms were shaking, and his chest was pounding. He was sweating through his shirt. Gary drove back to work, where he was almost useless for the rest of the day.

When men believe lies, their lives become lies.

The whole thing was a lie, a fantasy fabricated in Gary's mind. She was not flirting with him. She was not smiling at him to say, "Come and follow me." She did not want him in any sexual way. None whatsoever!

What made him do this? How could Gary, a Christian man, do this to his wife and two kids? How could he get so caught up in the drama of such a story, such a fantastic lie, that he became convinced that she wanted him? It was the power of fantasy, and the deception that things look better than they are, and it's the oldest trick in the book.

IT'S ALL LIES

In all of his wars, the enemy lies. The enemy will lie to your face. It is Satan's one basic tool.

Lie: *Expressing my sexuality is my greatest need, and only that can satisfy and fulfill me.*

Hollywood just seems to love perpetuating this lie. How many male characters in today's television shows and movies are motivated by trying to have sex with a gorgeous woman? Why do many movies portray men as either corny and bumbling wimps stuck in the friend zone, or smooth womanizers?

What about marketing? How many products are advertised with an implicit promise that if you use, buy, wear, or drive this thing, women will be attracted to you, and you will get sex—which seems to be the most important thing of all.

Because of the natural sexual drive in men's bodies, this lie can be easy to believe. But don't fall for it. Sex is a beautiful thing in the correct context, but it is not the most important thing.

Lie: *It's normal to lust, and get lost in the desire for pornography.*

We were created to know God and find fulfillment in His life. That's what is normal. Remember, God had said, "The day you eat of this tree you shall surely die." Satan told Eve, "Not 'you shall surely die.'" He lied. He took the exact words of God, as written in the Hebrew text, and merely put a negative in front of them. Adam and Eve ate, and so they died, spiritually. What do dead men need? Life. Satan lies to us and tells us that life can be found in the "feel good" of lust, pornography, and naked ladies. But that's not life; it's death. It has the potential to destroy us. Oh, it's titillating and exciting all right. Intoxicating. It's easy to get hooked on a lie that somewhere in all of this sexual activity we are going to find life. But it's a lie. Every man in the church who is struggling with his lust and fantasies will tell you that it is defeating his spiritual life and making him feel worthless before God.

The enemy promises that a little indulgence never hurt anyone. But immorality and impurity kill the heart of a man. The lies of the enemy lead to devastation and ruin:

> *The lips of an adulteress drip honey, and smoother than oil is her speech; but in the end she is bitter as wormwood.... Her feet go down to death, her steps take hold of [the grave]* (Proverbs 5:3-5, NASB).

Solomon is quite blunt about the personal emptiness of sexual sin:

> *On account of a harlot one is reduced to a loaf of bread* (Proverbs 6:26, NASB).

And a following proverb is frightening:

> *Suddenly he follows her [the adulteress] as an ox goes to the slaughter...until an arrow pierces through his liver...so he does not know that it will cost him his life* (Proverbs 7:22-23, NASB).

Good grief! It will cost you your life! Eventually, sex out of God's design is painfully destructive. It will lead you to spiritual ruin and possibly the death of your marriage. It will reduce you to a lifeless lump of dough. Illicit sex will slaughter you. It could cost you your future, your family, your business, your ministry, and even your life, for many have committed suicide over the shame of their sexual strongholds.

Remember that movie-star client in California? In his brokenness, he was able to acknowledge the lie: "I thought, if I were able to have sex with such a beautiful woman, then I will finally be satisfied." But then the man dropped his head and acknowledged, "It was never enough... never enough. I always wanted more." He cried and sobbed.

This was a man who lived out a crazy sexual fantasy, but discovered that it was never enough. The enemy had lied to him, and he bought it. Even when he could feel the emptiness, he could not quit. He was going to prove that the lie was true but he was always left empty. Now he sobbed in despair.

You may not ever want to have a thousand women. But you may have in your mind a certain woman, that one particular star, that one particular woman at work, at church, at school, and she has what it takes to send you to that place of fantasy and desire. You don't need a thousand women to buy the lie. You are buying the lie when you think that this one woman, alone, is going to satisfy you.

Remember King Solomon? As one of the richest men in the world too, he could have sex anytime he wanted, and with the most beautiful women in the world, from Egypt to Babylon and beyond. He had 700 wives and 300 female maids. Yeah, we know, to have sex with each of them once in one year, that would be two women every day, and three on the weekends and holidays. But he didn't start out his career accumulating all of these women. Oh, no. The earlier book Solomon wrote in the Bible is called Song of Songs, a beautiful and godly diary of Solomon and his wife, when they were two young lovers devoted to each other. He and his bride enjoyed the beauty and sensuality, romance and glory of sex as God intended. In the poetry of this book we read passages that hint of very erotic lovemaking scenes that include the tender touching and kissing of every part of the body. It is powerful.

But something was awakened in Solomon that he did not bridle and temper. According to the book of Ecclesiastes, the book that he obviously wrote after The Song of Songs, we see that Solomon bought the lie. His life became a life of hedonistic extremes. He gradually accumulated the other thousand women, along with a staggering amount of financial wealth, palaces, estates, and gardens that were the envy of the ancient world. But it was never enough! He always wanted more. Even the wisest man in the world was vulnerable to the enemy's lies.

Something happened in his heart, and it drove him from the wife of his youth. He turned from wisdom to folly and madness, to see what could satisfy the soul. He followed the lie, and the emptiness of his life got so bad that Solomon reached the point of despair. His life of wealth, fame and sex left him bitter and empty, so empty, that he even said, "I hate life." When any part of your life—your business, your investments, your vacations, your family life, your sexual life—is lived apart from God, it will become empty and emotionally painful. Solomon became so broken by the lie that he despaired of all the fruit of his accumulations that he had gained (see Ecclesiastes 2:20). The lies of the enemy drove Solomon toward suicide (see Ecclesiastes 2:17).

The lie will promise, but never fulfill. It will one day leave you empty. Look at Psalm 106, a psalm that retells the story of the Israelites wandering in the wilderness. God miraculously provided every day a mystery food called "manna." But there came a day that the children of Israel wanted more, and verse 14 says that they "craved intensely in the wilderness." That's the biblically polite way to say, "they were in a white-hot lust and burning with complaint against God for something that they wanted!"

So God gave them their request. Quail. But along with the quail, verse 15 says God sent a "wasting disease." A wasting disease? In the margin of your Bible you can see that the literal translation is, "leanness into their soul." It means that no matter how much they ate, they never got full. Their morbid appetite failed to appease their hunger. God gave them what they craved, but when they got it, the soul was never satisfied. In contrast to the lies about sex, here is a sober truth: *Physical lust can never be satisfied; the more you feed it, the hungrier it will become.*

The truth is, you are chasing after other lovers. You want something more than you want God. Here's the trouble. First, you are wiring your brain to always want more. Then when your spirit is not leading the soul in the work of spiritual transformation, the soul revolts and leads the spirit—and lust will reign! Your soul will always be hungry for more. Sounds just like our experience with lust, fantasy, and especially pornography, doesn't it? The more we take in, the more we want.

"Leanness of soul" is why we go back to the lie, over and over.

My soul craves sexual gratification through illicit intimacy (an adulterous act) or through false intimacy (pornography) or through simple monologue (my own lusts and fantasy).

But they never satisfy! I'm always left empty.

Renew your mind with this. Sexual sin will only produce more emptiness in the soul. Believe what fools have proven to be true!

It's folly to understand it. It's idolatry. Sex is an idol in our culture, and idols never satisfy. Idols leave you empty. That's why God told us not to have any.

Worse than being empty and unfulfilled, the lie perpetuates our spiritual immaturity. The study of sexual strongholds is, quite simply, a study in immaturity. *If you believe the lies, you remain trapped in immaturity; you never grow up into manhood.*

This is a brutal reality: If you believe lies, then you remain a child. If you live your life based on lies, then you will never grow up. This is a spiritual principle that young men are not often coached in. How do you grow up? You become a man of truth. Ephesians 4:15 (NASB) tells us that this is how we grow up: "Speaking the truth in love, we are to grow up in all aspects into Him...Christ."

You grow up by speaking the truth. Paul took the word for "truth" and stretched it into a word describing "a way of living," making a word that can be translated, literally, as "being a truth-er." We grow up by being a truth-er. We walk into maturity by getting out of the lies of our culture, and getting into being a man of truth.

Renew your mind with this. We grow up when we come clean before God. We are strengthened with our band of brothers or with our counselors, our pastors, and leaders. We mature when we begin to read the truth, receive the truth, believe the truth and speak the truth. We must live in the truth, and live with her truthfully. We must date women as truth-ers. No deceiving and defrauding her, no taking advantage of her. No more lying. No more secrets. No more hiding and covering up.

Don't start up any more secrets. Don't keep any more secrets. Behave on your dates, young men, as if you are dating the Father's daughter. You are! Behave around women as if your wife were present and watching. Be a man of integrity, of wholeness, with no secret compartments. No sneakiness. No duplicity. Period.

No man ever broke the power of lust and pornography, the power of sexual strongholds, without first becoming a truth-er.

When men believe lies, their lives become lies, and only the truth can set you free, especially the truth about your problem.

In a lot of ways, we have failed to grow up in the church. We have failed because the enemy's lies have kept us locked up in sexual immaturity. In this book, we hope we have given you so much more than a few behavioral tips, insights and strategies, techniques and tricks that you have tried before and that didn't work over the long haul.

It's time to live the Christian life we have never lived before.

Come out of the lies that you have bought, and renew your mind with these truths:

- The beauty of sex is in a relationship of bonding, connecting, and intimacy with the wife of your youth.

- Anything that has this much propensity for beauty, also has this much propensity for pain.

- The beauty of sex is only found within its God-ordained boundaries.

- We walk into maturity by getting out of the lies of our culture, and getting into being a man of truth.

- In the realm of illicit sex, it is only a deception to think that things look better than they are.

- Even a man of wisdom is vulnerable to the enemy's lies.

- The lie will promise, but never fulfill.

- When lust reigns, your soul will always be hungry for more.

- Lies perpetuate our spiritual immaturity.

C.S. Lewis reminded us that if we surrendered to all our desires and let our desires rule in life, it will lead to terrible consequences: impotence, disease, jealousies, lies, secrets, and everything that is the opposite of health, joy and honesty. He continued:

For any happiness in this world, quite a lot of restraint is going to be necessary.... For [sexual desire] will have to be controlled anyway, unless you are going to ruin your whole life.[44]

The lies of the enemy always harm. The lies about sex can ruin your life. That's the truth. Let the truth set you free. Galatians 5:1 says that it is for freedom that Christ has come to set us free!

Renew your mind with the truth. Resist the lies of the enemy. Stand firm in the maturity of being a truth-er. Press in to your relationships—with God, with Her (your wife or girlfriend), and with those closest to you. We are broken in relationships and we are healed in them.

QUESTIONS FOR REFLECTION OR DISCUSSION

1. Do you remember when you told your first lie?

2. Did you ever use a lie to avoid a negative reaction from someone else, like you father or mother, or your wife?

3. Did you ever lie to your parents about your sexual behavior?

4. Talk with your accountability group about the lies in culture about sexuality.

5. Are you a person who is capable of taking risks? With whom do you need to take a risk and tell the truth? Have someone hold you accountable to telling that truth.

---

44 C.S. Lewis, *Mere Christianity* (New York: Macmillan, 1960), 93.

11

ACCOUNTABILITY: WHY WE NEED IT TO WORK

*By definition, grace is something we can't
give ourselves. It comes from outside of us.
You must have relationship to grow.*
—HENRY CLOUD

*Two are better than one, because they
have a good return for their labor.*
—ECCLESIASTES 4:9

Donald arrived for his Friday morning men's Bible study running a little late, as usual. It had been a hectic week, and he hadn't gotten his shirt ironed the night before. Randy, the leader, had already finished the opening prayer as Donald came in the door and quietly took an empty chair at the long conference table. Randy's office was a quiet place at 6:45 in the morning. Coffee was ready, so Donald got back out of his chair and stepped over to the coffee table in the back of the room. He was thankful again this morning that it was in the back of the room, so he could get his coffee without disturbing Randy.

Randy announced, "Let's go around the room and check in with each other. How's it going, men? Anything we can pray about?"

Mario always seemed to speak up first. That was reasonable, seeing that his job was great, his wife was always loving and supporting, and his children too small to be in any trouble. A couple of the men would never admit it out loud, but they were envious of Mario's marriage. Who wouldn't be though, with sweet Laura? Everybody loved her.

Donald sank down in his chair with his coffee. He bowed his head to blow on his coffee, and help it cool before the first sip. A cup of coffee in your hands can help divert your eyes away from having to look at the other men. On this morning, Donald did not want to look at the other men. Randy wanted everyone to "check in" and report on their past week, and Donald wished he had not come this morning. But he knew he needed it. He had looked at porn on Wednesday night, and the guilt was felt anew as Mario finished bragging, er, well, finished checking in about how well things were going at home; and no, he didn't have any prayer requests, of course.

Eventually, it was Donald's turn. Here's how it went:

RANDY: Donald, how are you, buddy? How's the fight going?

DONALD: Well, it's been a tough week.

RANDY: Have you struggled this week?

DONALD: Well, yeah, you could say so.

RANDY: Did you struggle with porn this week?

DONALD: Yeah. I did look at it once this week.

(This is where we lose our notion of healthy accountability. This is where we throw men under the bus headed to Defeat Street. In the spirit of the law, we actually condemn a man to his shame, instead of help him into freedom.) It goes like this:

RANDY: I see, hmm, well, Donald, that's at least four or five weeks in a row now that you have looked at porn.

DONALD: I know. I know, it's just...it seems... I just keep struggling.

RANDY: Donald, you've asked us to keep you accountable.

At this point, Randy has that look of an exasperated father. His mouth shows a grimace, more because of his frustration with Donald than because he has any sympathetic pain for Donald. Randy's eyes go up in his head slightly, as he reveals his irritation with Donald.

RANDY: How are we going to hold you accountable if you won't work at it?

Donald feels a little heat on his neck. He can tell Randy is put out. Everyone else is silent. Then Craig speaks up.

CRAIG: Come on, Donald. Don't you want to be free? You don't seem to be trying at all? Actually, I think it's been at least six weeks in a row now.

Donald purses his lips, as he thinks to himself, *Well, just pile on, why don't you. Doesn't anybody understand how hard this is? Doesn't anybody else struggle with anything?*

RANDY: Well, Donald. We can't do it for you. If you want us to hold you accountable, I mean, what can we do? You've got to fight this thing. I don't think you're even fighting. Are you? I mean....

Donald can only keep his head down. All he feels is more shame and condemnation. It was true that he wanted to be held accountable, but he just can't seem to even accomplish one week of victory over the pornography. He feels like such a loser. He hates everything at the moment. He hates his job. He hates his struggle at the company. His wife is unsupportive, and she doesn't understand how hard he is working. Homelife is frustrating. He can't seem to get a break anywhere, and no one seems to care. He's starting to pull away emotionally from this group of men.

RANDY: Well, let's continue on with our Bible study this morning, and hopefully there will be some wisdom and insight for all of us.

There you have it. That's what we call Accountability. It's not very helpful, is it? Most of us men have been in some kind of follow-up group after the church men's retreat. We signed up on Saturday afternoon to join an "after group," and came home from the retreat motivated to "get after" the issues that the speaker had talked about.

It's putting on outward pressure to fix an inward condition, and accountability really doesn't work that way. It's kind of like a policeman. If the only time you hear from him is when he has pulled you over, confronting you to cite your speeding violation and write out a ticket, he is holding you accountable in a way, but he is not changing your desire to speed. He can shame you, frustrate you, and even scare you into tapping your brakes and slowing down. But if you love to speed, he cannot change your heart. He has no power to do that.

In our accountability groups we are to speak the truth in a spirit of love and gentleness. But often our group interactions can seem so fruitless. We have plenty of outward pressure, which often only appears to produce more shame, condemnation, and failure. Such efforts make for poor motivators.

ACCOUNTABILITY RENEWS BOTH OUR MINDS AND OUR EMOTIONS

If I am going to be held accountable, then I must have self-awareness. In the story above, Donald had no self-awareness. On his way to the computer at 10:30 at night to look at pornography, he was unaware of his thoughts and where his mind was. You can't renew your mind if you can't find your mind. You can't take thoughts captive to Christ, if you are unaware of your thoughts.

There is a theme we have been developing throughout this book. True, much of our sexual sin is the result of falling to temptation when we are enticed by our own lusts and desires (see James 1:14). However, some of our vulnerability to temptation comes because we have trained ourselves to go to sex for comfort. This is the area that has been the least examined in our Christian approach to sexual purity. So, let's repeat that point here as plainly as possible:

Some of the time we men are driven to sexual sin by painful thoughts and emotions.

We carry these painful thoughts and emotions in our hearts. When we get hurt in relationships, these injuries (betrayal, rejection, abandonment, etc.) have a profound effect on our core beliefs about ourselves. Of course, these core beliefs most often will be negative and damaging beliefs relative to the injury we experienced. Further, these beliefs will be attached to certain emotions. Thus, each time I remember the injury, each time that I dwell on the hurt, the same beliefs and their companion emotions will be stirred up in my heart, and the injury and the emotion will become attached to one another.

Painful beliefs about myself, when joined to such painful emotions, make it easy in the future to avoid relational intimacy. Who wants to get hurt like that, again?

What we believe about ourselves directly affects how we relate to other people. If I have been hurt in the past, then I will be cautious with love and intimacy in the future. As a result, my intimacy skills will not be developed into maturity, and I can more easily escape into porn because of the loneliness and because of the struggle I have in relating well to God and to significant others.

My first work, then, is to find out where my mind and emotions are. This work is what we would call "emotional self-awareness." We have misunderstood the role of emotions in the church, to the degree that we discount and devalue emotions. We speak of them almost as if they are evil. They are not. Our emotions can be trustworthy allies in the renewing of the mind.

What do our emotions do that is so trustworthy, you ask?

Our emotions give us a hint as to what we are thinking, because they are associated with our thoughts. When we are feeling the urge to look at pornography and self-sex, we must stop and analyze what is going on "under the hood." Something is driving us to seek out comfort or to "medicate" with the "happy chemicals" that run across the brain. We are often masking that pain, that is, we are altering the chemicals in our brains because we want to feel better. We discover that "under the hood" we are being driven by our painful thinking about ourselves.

Here's the point: *Some of us are caught up in sexual sins that are connected directly to our negative, painful thoughts and emotions about ourselves.* We have spent our teenage and young adult years coping with our painful feelings by using sex to medicate ourselves and feel better. Yet, we fail to see that much of our sexual behavior, outside *and* inside our marriage bed, is driven by this painful need to feel better, to get relief from the painful emotions and thoughts that come from events in our past that have nothing to do with sex!

As C.K. Chesterton has often been quoted: "We are destined to misunderstand the story that we find ourselves in."

If only we had a tool for helping us gather our thoughts and feelings, and discovering our core beliefs about ourselves.

We do, and it is called true accountability.

We need other people to listen to us talk. Yes, as we talk they listen to our decision-making processes, to discern the motivations and the intentions of our hearts. We need people to help us see and hear from God's Word and the leading of the Holy Spirit. We need feedback on what is going on inside of us when we make poor decisions. This is the true work of holding someone accountable. It is not shaming. Rather, it is liberating. We don't need a policeman. We need a listening friend, who will help us discover our thoughts as we take those thoughts captive to Christ.

This is where accountability partners can be helpful. You can talk with them about this "sexualization" of your hurtful past. You can talk to them about your childhood pain and emptiness. They can ask you questions to help you learn more about the connection and bond you have created between your childhood pain, your adult pain and your sexual strongholds. You cannot change or heal what you do not see. Accountability should include the process of us helping one another to "see" the connection between the triggers and decisions and sex, so that it can lead to change and healing.

STRATEGY
A good accountability partner can help with real-time prayer as tough situations arise. A simple text to your accountability partner saying "feeling triggered—please pray" gives you the strength of another person battling with you.

ACCOUNTABILITY IS ABOUT BREAKING UP THE ROUTINE

Second, accountability is when someone holds you to the truth. The truth will set you free. In this regard, accountability must never allow denial. Friends don't let friends say,

"I don't know *why* I did that."

"I don't know *why* I said that flirtatious thing to his wife."

"I don't know *how* I ended up driving to that end of town."

"I don't know *how* I ended up looking at porn last night."

Such statements are a cop-out. It is living in denial. An accountability partner must never join in the false belief that bad behavior is out of our control, or that our bad behavior just came out of nowhere, from out of left field or just out of the blue, as we might say. Accountability partners must help us recognize this truth about our sexual sin: *It has a ritual element to it. We do the same thing over and over. Therefore, we know exactly what we're doing!*

As we said above, all behavior has a backstory. Every time we act out in our sexual struggle it is deliberate and intentional, and often driven by our past. Here's why:

1. All behavior starts with the *thought* about that behavior. That is, I looked at porn at 10:30 P.M. because the *thought* of looking at porn hit me at 5:45 P.M. on my drive home. The *thought* arose because some event or episode in daily life triggered the thought. It can be triggered by lust, by your secretary's cleavage, or by getting a sexually inappropriate email from someone. Or it can be triggered by stress at work, conflict at the sales meeting, or simply an idle moment during which you recalled a painful, shameful event from years earlier.

2. As teenagers we "sexualized" the *thoughts* of our backstory. Each time we experienced one of these frustrating events or episodes in daily life, it is easy to turn to self-sex. Today, frustrating events trigger the *thought* to look at porn or turn to self-sex as a form of comfort or medication. Thus, these "triggered thoughts" become fantasies at 5:45 P.M., obsessions by 7:15 P.M., and preoccupations around 9:30 P.M., until I look at porn at 10:30 P.M. Bad stuff happens, and our minds go to sex! Why? Because the brain's wiring got mixed this way.

3. However, before the *thoughts* lead to actual sexual behavior, there are many preliminary steps in between. Before someone actually looks at porn, he has to carve out time in the day to do it. He has to arrange his schedule to accommodate it. You have to make an excuse to leave the office. You have to go to lunch alone. You have to download the porn earlier and store it on a private, secret flash drive. You have to have secret passwords. You have to arrange to have more work to do at the office later tonight. You have to start a fight with your wife to get her to go

to bed early. You have to go online to research where to get an escort in another town. You have to groom that attractive, new woman in the office building that you see occasionally.

There are a thousand small steps we take on the way to the crime scene! All of this is called *ritual,* and there are a thousand different rituals for a thousand men. Everyone has his own game. If you want to be held accountable, you must invite your listening friend into your rituals. Your friend must get into the patterns of your story, expose the rituals, and help you see them. Accountability breaks the routine. *Intervene in the routine! Disrupt the ritual cycle by removing its secrecy and cover.*

Our rituals are propped up and supported by various ways of deceptive thinking, too. We need accountability to confront our faulty ways of thinking. God created us to be "truth-ers," and we mature by walking in truth:

> *Behold, you delight in truth in the inward being...* (Psalm 51:6, ESV).

> *Speaking the truth in love, we are to grow up...* (Ephesians 4:15, ESV).

Accountability partners need to help us see the deceptive schemes of the enemy, which keep us trapped in immaturity and locked in our rituals. Though this will require you to be vulnerable over and over, *it is going to help you!* While most of us continue to hide out in our secrecy, we also do not grow spiritually by keeping our secrets. This difficult work is going to take you where you have never gone before, uncovering the schemes you have been hiding behind. Consider the power of the following questions to uncover your schemes.

- Do I just "hear" the Word, but never do it? (See James 1:22.)

- Am I spiritualizing and not calling my sin for what it is? (See 1 John 1:8.)

- Am I rationalizing that I will not reap what I sow? (See Galatians 6:7.)

- Am I thinking that my behavior is not corrupting me? (See 1 Corinthians 15:33-34.)

- Is my thinking a form of denial?

- Is my thinking a form of fantasy?

- Is my thinking producing a pattern of avoidance and withdrawal?

- Is my thinking a form of rationalization? Spiritualization? Intellectualization? Sexualization?

If we are going to have accountability in our lives, we must have perceptive and spiritually intuitive friends who can see and read between the lines. Our rituals are built around our thoughts, and these thoughts function as filters keeping us from perceiving the truth. Thus, instead of seeing the truth, we actually filter it out! We need accountability partners who have healthy filters, who can see the truth, and help us see where we are missing it. This process can be stimulated if together we can ask, "Where did I learn to think this way?" and "Is this thinking a problem?"

Consider this sequence: "When did porn and/or self-sex become a coping strategy in life? Is it possible I was coping with difficulty in my home at that time? What was happening back then? Who hurt me? Who was I hurting? What lie did I buy? What attitude did I adopt? What truth from God's word is the antidote for this ritual/belief? What identity do I want to believe? Who do I want to be when I am triggered in the future?"

Accountability Requires the Right Kind of Men Around You

Third, true accountability is seven days a week. There is no time off for good behavior. For Pete's sake, good behavior is your goal! Don't be surprised by it, and then reward yourself with a little bit of porn! Remember, good behavior is laying down that strong, new muscle movement! New behaviors should lay the groundwork for strengthening our ability to resist triggers in the future. God always wants to work His work of deliverance in us. Every day. So let's give Him plenty of obedience to work with.

At least 40 times, the New Testament uses the words "one another" or "each other." God has had accountability in mind from the beginning. He put us together for this. Hell wants to get us alone, and keep us alone! Men, we are not that strong. We need a team, a band of brothers. We really doubt that you are going to win this battle alone.

Remember the battle in Exodus 17, where the Israelites were at war with the Amalekites? The army of God prevailed as long as Moses could hold up the staff of God. But he couldn't keep doing it without help. Victory in the battle depended on Moses' having others to hold him up. If you undertake this battle alone, you will go mad. Fighting solo doesn't ever work. When you fight alone, you go mad alone, and you die alone.

You need healthy relationships around you to help you. Without support, you will fail. You will always need somebody to talk to, someone to call, someone to pray with you. You are going out to battle, with a target on your back, and if you are alone, it's as though you are going out with only a water pistol in your hand. You don't have anyone on your flank! You don't have anyone watching your back! There is power in knowing that you have someone in your life who sees you when you succeed and when you fail, but loves you still.

Not just anybody, though. Be wise in whom you choose. Speak to someone who will work this plan with you. Find someone who will be faithful. Find someone who will show up. Some leaders are too busy for you. Don't bother them. Find a band of brothers, but get a point man. Get the one man who loves you, but the one who will love you enough to be firm and bold with you. Get someone who is with you and around you during the week, someone who can hold you accountable in your speech and in your relationship with your wife, and who also has a chance to see your behavior around other women. Get someone who understands how God truly sees you and has his own foundation in God's word.

Accountability Helps You Do What You Have Never Done Before

This is not just about reminding you of *what not to do*. It is about encouraging you to be the man that God has called you to be. When Jonathan came alongside David, the Scripture says that Jonathan "strengthened his hand in God" (1 Samuel 23:16, ESV). Accountability partners remind you that you are a beloved son of God, that you are fearfully and wonderfully made, that God has forgiven you, and that by His life in you, you can overcome. Accountability groups remind you to be the spiritual leader of your home, even when those you love, like your wife, are not always encouragers. We need other men to encourage us to step up and remain patient, kind and loving. We will need them to see the man of God that we can be—sometimes even before we see it ourselves. We will need the men in our accountability groups to remind us daily of this calling.

Accountability is a "one another" relationship that helps you do what you have never done before. It involves friendships that strengthen you to step into a future you have never lived before. You step into a future when you live in the power and authority of Christ's life in you. You have never lived there in regard to your sexual strongholds. You have kept your sexual mind firmly on the earth and in your past. Accountability helps you learn from the immediate future, as His life emerges underneath your new steps of Spirit-filled discipline and freedom.

John Wooden has a quote that sums up this chapter well, *"Failure* is not fatal, but *failure* to change might be."[45] We are all going to fail. That's a given. Out of our failure, let's get a band of brothers around us who are going to help us. Let's receive from these men, and let's be mature enough to let it bring forth a change in our lives.

Don't wait until temptation strikes. Always be found working on your issues. Temptation is coming, so in the meantime always be building your spiritual and relationship muscles. Be developing healthy intimacy with

---

45 John Wooden, *A Lifetime of Observations and Reflections On and Off the Court* (New York: McGraw-Hill, 1997), 96.

God, with yourself (self-awareness, remember?), intimacy with your wife and children, and intimacy with a group of accountability partners. Plan your plan, and plan on keeping it. Make phone calls to reach out for help, attend meetings, ask for grace as you read Scripture and pray, turn to God and others when the triggers come, and even plan on avoiding the places and situations which will cause triggers. Do these things. Do them daily. Do them for as long as necessary.

If you continue to struggle, then accountability will need to challenge you to seek more professional help. There is no shame in that. God uses them for your good.

Accountability Allows an Outlet for Your Story

As we trace the life of Jesus and His teaching, we see that He loved to use parables (stories) to help people understand the truth. There is something powerful and healing when we come to understand the story we find ourselves in. To tell our story is to give our testimony, and in the process God can begin a healing movement in our lives that leads to victory.[46] *Our story has a way of revealing the clues needed to overcome sexual struggles.* Most of us don't realize that. We also don't realize that God wants to meet us in our story. He wants to become part of our narrative in order to heal and transform us.

God is a storyteller. Take the Old Testament, for example. It's the true story of one family and how God promised that He would bless them, and then bless the world through them. It's an amazing story of God's love and provision, but it is also a story filled with betrayal, lies, treachery, and war, not to mention adultery, incest, rape, and prostitution, fueled by unforgiveness, revenge, bitterness, and murder. The Old Testament is filled with stories like our lives. Our life stories are often characterized by betrayals, lies, anger, rage, unforgiveness, and bitterness. Our stories are filled with these behaviors and attitudes, and the emotional pain they

---

46 We realize that Rev 12:11 ("They triumphed over him by the blood of the Lamb and by the word of their testimony") has a particular eschatalogical context; but, as counselors, we cannot help but notice that these words can powerfully apply to our present-day lives in the counseling context, and are a worthy formula for spiritual growth and healing.

cause, and sexual ways of coping. Understanding our stories can be the beginning of getting freedom at last.

God wants us to understand our stories; that we might be saved from our story.

How do we know God wants us to understand our story? Because very often when He shows up in the Bible to talk to humans, He is asking them questions, meeting them in their stories! God's first spoken words to a human being took the form of a question, *"Adam, where are you?"* He was asking Adam to tell Him what had happened. *"What's the story, Man?"* It wasn't that God didn't know what had happened. He wanted Adam to explain it, because if Adam didn't understand his own story, then God was going to help him understand it. Then Adam would know what God already knew.

In the Gospels, there is an account of Jesus teaching a woman to find healing and peace by inviting Him into her story. It's the famous story of a woman whose name we never knew. She is simply called "the woman at the well," and her story is found in chapter 4 of the Gospel of John.

Jesus and his disciples were on the long hike from Jerusalem to the area of the Sea of Galilee. They stopped for lunch halfway on that journey in a region called Samaria. The Samaritans were a mixed race, half-Jew and half-Gentile, which put them on the wrong side of the law of Moses, which forbade mixed marriages. Outside the city of Sychar in Samaria was an historic water well. Jesus sat down alone to rest there, and sent all 12 disciples into the city to get something for lunch.

While He was alone at the well around the noon hour, a Samaritan woman came to draw water. Jesus asked her for a drink, and she wondered why a Jew would be asking her for a drink, or even willing to use the water pot of a Samaritan.[47] This is a woman with a diminished identity, a woman in need of healing. She has a "story" of shame that began at

---

47   Her vocabulary appears to be referring to Jewish scruples that since Samaritan women were ceremonially unclean, so were their utensils, including water pots. Leon Morris, "The Gospel According to John," *New International Commentary on the New Testament (NICNT)* (Grand Rapids, MI: Eerdmans, 1971), 259.

birth; she's a Samaritan, less than a Jew and a woman, less than a man. Responding to Jesus, she immediately yields herself to her shame.

Jesus knew that there was more going on with this woman. The noon hour was late in the morning to obtain water, for women of a village would usually come first thing in the morning to get their water for daily use. *What's up with that? Was she avoiding the other women? Was she sleeping late? Did her sins keep her up at night? Did she have something to hide? Was she ashamed of her story? Was she hiding her "stuff"?*

His heart went out to this broken and ashamed woman, and Jesus let her know that He had something she might want. Jesus told her that if she knew who He was, she would ask *Him* for a drink and He would give her "living water." Everyone who would drink of the well water would be thirsty again, but whoever would drink of the living water would never be thirsty again (see John 4:10-14).

When the woman asked for this water, Jesus went for her heart. He said to her, "Go and get your husband and come here" (see verse 16). Jesus went for her "story," and He got it.

"I have no husband" (John 4:17).

Jesus helped her into honesty, "I know. What's true is that you've had five husbands, and presently you are just living with a man" (see verses 17-18).

Now there's a story shot through and through with rejection and disgrace! (Although today, it doesn't sound far-fetched in our pop-star culture.) This woman's story was full of pain and shame. Look at what we can discern from these few verses:

She is a Samaritan by birth (defiled by cultural Jewish standards).

She has been married five times.

She has been divorced five times.

She must be an adulteress, for something has caused all five husbands to "put her away."

She is now living with a man, unmarried.

Under Jewish law, a woman could not divorce her husband; therefore, her behavior had to have been so bad that it led five husbands to "put her away." And where did this sixth man come from? Was he divorced, too? Had he abandoned his wife to be with her? Talk about a story of rejection. Talk about public humiliation. This is a story about adultery, failure, brokenness, and pain. This woman's shame comes from far more than simply being a mixed-race Samaritan woman.

Given this level of pain and shame, here was a woman with a spiritual thirst. She was thirsty for love and acceptance. She was thirsty for forgiveness, but she couldn't receive it until she came clean with her need for it! She needed to exchange her story for His story (see Romans 6:3-7).

Immediately, she felt the discomfort of being so honest, so she tried to change the topic to worship. She tried to hide behind religion! Jesus allowed the conversation to go there, but He brought it back to the heart of the matter, telling her, "true worshipers will worship the Father in the Spirit and in truth" (John 4:23).

This portrays a powerful posture that can help tear down sexual challenges. *Either you live in the Spirit and in truth as you walk with God in your story, or you live in the flesh and in falsehood as you walk around God and ignore your story.*

Walk in your story or ignore your story. One leads to healing and grace. The other leaves you stuck.

Many Samaritans came out to the well and believed in Jesus Christ as Messiah and Savior; they "believed in him because of the woman's testimony" (John 4:39). The woman, who had been so filled with shame, actually went on to share her story! What was once shrouded in shame was now a celebration that He, the Son of God, knew her. Her story was no longer something to hide from in shame. She had told Him her story, and Jesus Christ had stepped into the middle of it. He had affirmed that forgiveness, acceptance, and the love of God were free for people with a story like hers. He gave her living water.

Understanding your own story is the beginning of healing and freedom. You are as sick as your secrets.

Talking to God and walking through your story with Him (and, as needed, a trusted friend, pastor, or professional Christian counselor) is how you learn where your story went awry. You will start to see more clearly where you got off track, where you got hurt and broken, and where your missteps and sins became costly.

Understanding, walking, and praying through your story is how you come to see whether unforgiveness and bitterness are still in your heart. You find out whether lustful emotional ties still exist, and whether you have "unfinished business" with your former schoolmates, your mother, your father, your ex-wife, with God or with yourself.

When you know your story, you understand your anger, your bitterness, your shame, and your stubbornness. You realize your own sinful steps, and the sins that others did against you. Then you know where you need insights, wisdom, and the transformational grace and healing comfort of the Lord Jesus Christ. Your story holds the clues as to why you are struggling with sexual strongholds.

We know that most men are not comfortable with revealing their lives. Many a man has declined an invitation to join a men's group at church, and for good reason, due to the fear that there will be small group discussion and that "I'll have to tell my stuff, and I don't want other men knowing my stuff. That's stupid!" But everyone's got stuff. Your "stuff" is your story; it's the "unfinished business" you carry in your heart. Your stuff is the source for so many of your problems, such as why your wife is so unhappy or your son is mad at you. But especially, your stuff is at the heart of your sexual battle.

We are *not* talking about your getting up behind the pulpit and blabbing your story to the whole congregation. Absolutely not! That's not productive. That's not safe. Start with the Lord.

You might say, "I have!"

Great! Continue doing it. Remember His promise that if you will turn over your sin, He will be faithful and just to forgive you and to cleanse you from all unrighteousness (see 1 John 1:9). Let Him and others into your story. The unhealthy patterns become lifelong and your life will get confusing and stuck, unless you find "another" to come alongside to help you understand and work through your story.

Jesus wants to enter your story. But it's not so He can shame you more. It's not because He's mad at you. He wants to meet you there. He wants to bring grace and truth to your story. It's for *freedom* that Christ has come to set you free (see Galatians 5:1).

When you experienced pain and discomfort growing up, you found a way to cope, but most of your coping was unhealthy and sinful. Now it's time to solve the puzzle of your life, to understand what drives your sexual behavior—to redeem those puzzle pieces. God can help you to identify those painful puzzle pieces and He will alter them with His presence, His life. However, in order to experience healing you have to prayerfully and purposefully talk and work through the hurts of your story. Your ability to overcome your sexual conflicts will depend on the work that you do to understand and heal the pain and the patterns of your life. *God is calling you into dialogue.*

Now, we must acknowledge that pain doesn't drive everyone. The reason some men are trapped in sexual strongholds is because they grew up thinking that they were, well, a "Junior Master of the Universe."[48] Yes, sometimes the reason for unhealthy sexual behavior is simply charisma and moxie that women are strongly attracted to. This can put a man in the company of broken and needy young ladies who are confused about love and sex. "Love" and sex come kind of naturally. As a result, drawn by his own lusts and addicted to the "chemical high," he enters high school and/or college with a sexual prowess not shared by all of his peers. All of the attention given to sex in the world around him, and all of the competition led him to get lost in it. And those unhealthy patterns can continue even into a marriage, robbing it of the beauty of what God intended for pleasure and intimacy.

It's all there somewhere in our stories. God often finds us lost in or ignoring our story. Adam was hiding, and we hide, too. We hide *in* our stories, telling people only part of our story. We hide *behind* our stories,

---

48   See Patrick Carnes, *Don't Call It Love* (New York: Bantam, 1992), 184ff.

creating false stories so that people won't know who we really are. We hide *from* our stories, acting as if we don't have a story.

God is always asking questions, because He made us for intimacy with Him, and that intimacy comes through dialogue. The sins that we cover, He uncovers. The sins that we uncover, He covers (see Proverbs 28:13).

Why does God meet us in our broken places? Because He's in our stories already. Don't be afraid of Him. He wants us to acknowledge Him there.

EPILOGUE: ACCOUNTABILITY AT THE MEN'S BIBLE STUDY

Let's go back to Donald. Imagine that he showed up to his Friday morning group with this new way of accountability and found grace, support, and acceptance. Here's how accountability might look:

RANDY: Donald, how are you, buddy? How's the fight going?

DONALD: Well, it's been a tough week.

RANDY: Have you struggled this week?

DONALD: Well, yeah, you could say so.

RANDY: Did you struggle with porn?

DONALD: Yeah. I did look once this week.

RANDY: Well, let's explore what happened, and see if we can help you figure it out. What night did you look at the porn?

DONALD: It was, uh, Wednesday night, I think. Yeah, Wednesday night.

RANDY: Ok. What was Wednesday like? What did you do that day?

DONALD: Well, I don't know. I don't remember much.

JERRY: Wait, haven't you mentioned before that Wednesday mornings are your sales meetings?

DONALD: Yeah, that's right.

RANDY: Ah ha! So, how were your numbers on Wednesday?

DONALD: Hmmmm. Good question. It's been a tough quarter. My numbers are not good, and they have not been good for at least five of the past six weeks. It's been bad.

CRAIG: Well, wait. Wouldn't that be a clue, you know, one clue as to why you looked at porn that night? You were feeling defeated, or frustrated, or something like that, huh?

DONALD: Yeah. Yeah, you're right. The meeting definitely ruined my afternoon [laughs].

MARIO: And wait! A few months ago you mentioned that you think your sales manager has it out for you, or something like that. I know you've talked about him before in here. What's the story, again?

DONALD: Yeah, he's one of those people-eaters,...can be pretty rough on people. Come to think of it, Wednesday morning, I felt like he was really put out with me and my numbers. But everybody's numbers are low this quarter. The economy for our industry has been bad.

RANDY: Yeah, but it's that feeling you got. You received it. You felt like he was disapproving of you, and you received the message: "I'm a failure." Would you agree?

DONALD: Yeah, I did.

JERRY: What did you do after the meeting? Do you remember? That will tell us.

DONALD: Yeah, I remember that I left the office and went driving around. Just wanted to get away.

JERRY: Where did you drive? Where did you go?

DONALD: Oh, my gosh. Now I remember. I went down Sixth Street. I mean, it was only 10:30, and there were no prostitutes on the street, but I shouldn't have been there. I have to confess, I used to go there during the summers when I was home from college, a buddy and I. We would chat with girls on the street, but never do anything. I remember now that I thought about those summer nights as I drove the street Wednesday morning, and I'm ashamed to say, well, it was arousing.

RANDY: Donald, we love you. But now you see that you were into a ritual by choosing to drive down Sixth Street. Driving that street was a way of escape. But it was also a way of stirring up the "feel good" chemicals in your brain, to escape the pain of the sales meeting. Do you see that?

DONALD: Yes. I see that. You are right. Oh, my gosh, I feel so stupid.

CRAIG: Don't go there. That's your shame-based identity. You're not stupid. You were struggling with your sense of failure. Your sales manager only stirred that up.

RANDY: And probably affected the kind of attitude you took home. What was your evening like. Can you remember? How did you find Melissa's attitude when you got home? Think back.

[Silence]

RANDY: Think about your routine? What are Wednesdays like at your house? Do the boys have ball practice that afternoon? Does Emily have gymnastics?

DONALD: Oh, yeah. Yeah, I remember, by the time Melissa came home with the kids, she was in a bad mood. Emily was crying, too. Yeah, the boys were back in their room, but Emily was doing her whining thing in the kitchen when I walked in, as Melissa was rushing to get dinner ready. She reminded me, again, that Wednesday nights would be a good night for one of us to pick up something on the way home. Why don't I ever think about that, she said. "It would be helpful," she said, "if you could remember just one thing I ask of you!" Yeah, that's right. We got into it right there in the kitchen, while Emily was still whining on the floor. Gee, now that I recall it all, we had a miserable evening. It was no fun at our home that night.

JERRY: There you go. Do you get it? You were in a funk. You were feeling like a failure at work. You went out and got aroused with sexual urges. Then you felt like a failure all afternoon. You come home and your wife reminds you that you're a failure as a leader of the household, one of your children is making you miserable, too. Your pump is primed, man! You are on a dead man's march toward pornography by 10:30 that night! I know that story. It happened to me plenty when my kids were that young.

CRAIG: All right, then. I'm going to call you every Wednesday morning and pray with you before the sales meeting. I'm going to help you set your mind on Christ.

RANDY: And I will call you every Wednesday afternoon, find out how the sales meeting went, what kind of mind-set you are in, and pray with you for a positive, spiritual evening at home with your family.

MARIO: Yeah, brother. We are going to help get you out of those painful thoughts and emotions. That's how you can break the cycle of pornography. You're gonna' do it, by the life of Christ in you.

Do you see how this will work better for Donald? His friends are helping him analyze his Wednesday. Their questions are exposing the thoughts and emotions that Donald was accumulating during the day. Their conversation becomes therapeutic and spiritual as they empower Donald to see the connection between his sense of failure and his urge for pornography, to understand that he was using sex as a comfort, a medication, for the emotional pain of the day. Thus, Donald was able to see what was "driving" him. This awareness, along with Scripture, renews both his mind and his emotions. Further, their questions and observations expose his rituals, thus giving him more power in the future to see them for himself. He has a better chance of resisting the urge to look at porn when he can realize that it is his sales manager that is the "trigger." Once Donald's accountability partners have helped him reach this understanding, Donald can start to invite God into his thoughts and actions *before* he is triggered and *during* his most tempting moments. (Connecting the sales manager with the urge to feel good sexually—now, there's an appalling thought!)

This is accountability that is truly helpful. A conversation like this helps someone like Donald see what he has never seen before, walk where he has never walked before, and break through spiritually to a place he has never been before.

QUESTIONS FOR REFLECTION OR DISCUSSION

1. Check the resource section of the back of the book for a list of websites that can help you find groups.

2. Talk to your pastor or local Christian counselor to see if they know of any support groups that are meeting in your area.

3. If there is no group to attend, then get one of the workbooks listed in the resource section, and start your own group, enlisting the pastor's help and the church's willingness to provide space for such a group.

12

YADA, YADA, YADA!

A young man today, in this whirling social cosmos,
chased by sins, fretted by doubts, has still one
sight which God sends him eternally; the sight
which Adam saw when he awoke from sleep.
—G.K. Chesterton

Adam knew Eve his wife, and she conceived....
—Genesis 4:1, esv

It is more than interesting, in light of our discussions on the brain, ruts, and strongholds, to see that God's chosen term for sex in the Old Testament was "to know." In Hebrew, it is pronounced *yadah,* and it means *knowing* information that is gained by the five senses. This word is used of God's knowledge of man as well man's knowledge of God—and, fascinatingly, *yadah* is used as the expression for sexual intercourse in marriage.

In using "to know" for sexual intercourse, God was signaling something to us in ancient times that only in the past 50 years or so has become evident to us through discoveries of neuroscientists: *To have sex with someone is to know that person.*

It is "knowledge" because during sex, the brain is receiving data and storing it, releasing chemicals and bonding, creating images, producing exhilaration and a high, as well as photocopying the images and storing them. While adrenaline is being released in the body, the brain releases its own form of adrenaline, norepinephrine, the hormone (chemical) that helps form and store memories. So it is the chemicals that are creating the "knowing" of your bride as you lie with her in naked glory.

Along with the other chemicals that are associated with sexual arousal, oxytocin binds your brain to the object in front of your eyes. If that's your wife, great! You are "knowing" her in a mind-altering, exhilarating way, with your brain in a chemical bath of bonding chemicals. Since God had all of that brain activity in mind when He created us, no wonder He called sex "knowing."

This is one reason why God wants to protect the act of marriage. It is because there is an actual physical bond created with anyone that we are naked and sexual with. God desires that sex only be with one's wife; thus, when God said through Moses, that a "man shall cleave to his wife" it was not merely a figure of speech. This cleaving is a literal bonding. The act of love, romance, and sex creates a chemical reaction in the brain that quite literally bonds a man and woman together.

Therefore, it would be wise advice (fathers, tell your sons!) that on your honeymoon night you do not have sexual intercourse in total darkness. Your eyes need to look at one another, so that the bonding is established with those first, glorious moments of sexual ecstasy. Did you realize that we humans are the only species on the planet that can have sex face to face? It's by design. So, open your eyes. Drink in her beauty. For God has designed that your brain, making use of that visual data, will create an actual soul-tie to your wife, and it will help you cleave to the wife of your youth.

This gives fresh insight to the proverb: *"Rejoice in the wife of your youth.... Let her breasts fill you at all times with delight; be intoxicated always in her love* (Proverbs 5:18-19).

Now you realize the power of that statement! When you gaze upon your wife's breasts, when you are aroused by her, when you touch her, when you make love to her, your brain is experiencing the same chemicals of euphoria as the man who is in a similar state from the use of drugs or alcohol. The chemicals triggered in the brain during sex are the chemicals of intoxication. God designed us biologically so that every man can "bond" with his wife, "knowing" her with his eyes, his heart, his brain, and with every cell in his body that is under the influence of those chemicals! This is the physical purpose of marriage in God's economy—to know and bond to one another, and to become "one body" (see 1 Corinthians 6:16).

Spiritually, there is something else going on with sex. There is a oneness being created spirit to spirit between husband and wife. When Adam and Eve made love to one another for the very first time in the Garden of Eden, we can imagine that every animal in the Garden bowed their head in awe. It was too beautiful. Even the angels could not have imagined the beauty of what God had created in the sexual union of the Man and the Woman. God was both present and pleased.

When Adam and Eve were holding one another in the ecstasy of their first sexual embrace, the Trinity in heaven must have been smiling with approval. The Father, Son, and Holy Spirit knew that the sexual union of husband and wife was a picture of the future relationship that They would have with us in the new covenant. The Apostle Paul spoke to this point when he wrote:

> *"Therefore a man shall leave his father and mother and hold fast to his wife, and the two shall become one flesh." This mystery is profound, and I am saying that it refers to Christ and the church* (Ephesians 5:31-32, ESV).

But while it made the Triune God smile with approval, Satan saw it, too. He saw The Man and the Woman in their sexual embrace, but instead of being caught up in the awesome power of the moment, he glanced toward Heaven. He saw the Trinity smiling, and Satan must have vowed in his dark heart that if God created sex with such beauty inherent in it, then he (Satan) would do everything in his power to destroy its beauty and goodness. Ever since, he has been doing everything in his power to defile and destroy the spiritual beauty of sexual intimacy.

What makes sex so beautiful is not the physical act alone, but the relational and spiritual intimacy that envelops the relationship. When the relationship is built on trust and connection, it includes emotional harmony, peace, and security. When the relationship is centered on the spiritual dimension of a shared relationship with God, then sex is wonderful. Built as it is on the chemical bonding of emotional and spiritual intimacy, it is satisfying to the soul. Sex is made to be the capstone of a healthy emotional, relational, and spiritual intimacy. Physical intimacy will always be more satisfying when it is experienced as the reward for, and the joyous expression of, the more important work of connecting and bonding.

Sex can be such a life-giving expression between husband and wife. But it turns to chaos and brokenness when we violate the design of God. Proverbs tells us that the violations lead to Hell! (See Proverbs 5:3-5.) What a sobering thought. Sex outside of marriage can take you to a place where sex becomes life taking instead of life giving. It is so powerful that I can get lost in it, overwhelmed and broken by it.

The key to sexual freedom is relationship. Sexual freedom is born in the beauty of relational intimacy—connecting and bonding, then coming together physically. Lust and pornography destroy such intimacy. They are never about love. In fact, lust and pornography defile the brain so badly that they have the power to kill love and kill relationship. Remember what we said early on, that anything with this much propensity for beauty has this much propensity for pain and brokenness.

This idea leads to a second way that Satan is destroying the beauty of intimate sex, and he is doing this in the church. We still acknowledge that sex is an appetite, one of our God-given human drives. Marriage has been given by God for the physical enjoyment of both man and wife. But if we build a doctrine on the belief that a woman must "give herself" physically to her husband for sex, anytime he wants it, regardless of her own emotional and spiritual discomfort at the moment, then we are violating true, godly submission. Especially if he has been a disrespecting, unloving boor toward her all evening! Then his sexual advances are hurtful to intimacy. Her yielding under such circumstances would not be submission. Perhaps it sounds more like bondage.

When we treat our wives as sex objects, or objectify them in any other way, when we *take* from them, even claiming that it is their biblical duty, our sexual experience is no longer an expression of love. In other words, when sex in the Christian bedroom is merely an act of self-gratification—when sex is for satisfying the man's physical drive alone—then he is violating the bonding, the connecting, the act of marriage.

Additionally, many women have been taught, wrongly, that it is not only a woman's duty to be available no matter what, but that she is responsible to make sure that her husband is so satisfied he will never stray from the marriage. First Corinthians 7:5 says "Do not deprive each other except perhaps by mutual consent and for a time, so that you may devote yourselves to prayer. Then come together again so that Satan will not tempt you because of your lack of self-control." This does not mean that the wife is responsible for satisfying the unmeetable needs of a man whose sexual drive and behaviors are impacted by his lust and pornography usage. His faithfulness is not her responsibility! A husband is responsible for managing his own adulteries of the heart. His heart is not his wife's responsibility.

Biologically, our brains can adjust to any change in the routine of sex. When your wife goes through menopause and her sex life gets put on "pause," then you have the duty to slow down your own sex drive, live with your wife in an understanding way, and cool your jets. Remember the wedding vows: better or worse, richer or poorer, in sickness or in health. You made a commitment to be with this woman and support and acknowledge her current needs. The Holy Spirit living in you can enable your heart and mind to do that, and your physiological state will make its own adjustment.

You are to live with your wife as if she were a piece of fine china. In First Peter 3:7 we read, "Husbands, in the same way be considerate as you live with your wives, and treat them with respect as the weaker partner and as heirs with you of the gracious gift of life, so that nothing will hinder your prayers"—and that very much includes your sexual relationship with her. This is a great question to ask yourself if you are feeling as though your prayers are bouncing off the ceiling and not being heard. How are you treating your wife? Are you loving her as a person? In your sexual life? You are to bring your sexual life under submission to Christ as your Head and accommodate yourself to your wife's physical, chemical, and emotional changes. Sex is not of supreme importance; love trumps sex. Love trumps your sexual drive. Your sexual pace and frequency must be subject to your wife's emotional and physical condition. We must preserve the emotional and spiritual intimacy above all else.

Are you developing your spiritual relationship with God and with your wife? Do you have a spiritual journey to share with each other? Do you grant her the "grace of life"? (See First Peter 3:7.) If you are growing deeper in the disciplines of the Christian life (walking the talk, as we say), if you are living from your heart and not from your theological head, then the door is open for God to transform you into a man who reflects His life. Then your wife, if she is healthy too, will respect you. Women desire to be intimate with men that they respect! In your marriage relationship, your physical intimacy level will never be separate from the safety and emotional intimacy in your relationship. Your sex life cannot rise above any existing dynamics of fear, or anger, between you.

QUESTIONS FOR REFLECTION OR DISCUSSION

1. What sexual messages do you carry with you from a variety of sources (family, school, culture, church)? How did your father talk to you about sex? What sermons or teachings have you heard about sex? Based on this history, share with your spouse your sense of God's plan of sexuality.

2. Read First Corinthians 7:5. Would you be willing to contract with your wife to take physical sex out of the relationship for a time so that you and she can devote yourself to prayer, meditation, Bible study, etc.? Then when you do come back together, your sex can be an expression of spiritual knowing and not just biology.

13

TAKING BACK THE GROUND AND HOLDING IT

*And though this world with devils filled should
threaten to undo us, we will not fear, for God
has willed His truth to triumph through us.*

—MARTIN LUTHER ("A Mighty Fortress Is Our God")

If you get one thing out of this book, make sure you grasp of the fact that you are in a war; you have an enemy. He is a very real enemy. He is alive and well and active in the affairs of men. In fact, he is profoundly influencing them. The god of this age is none other than Satan and his system of principalities and powers. The Apostle Paul wrote:

> *For our struggle is not against flesh and blood, but against the rulers, against the authorities, against the powers of this dark world and against the spiritual forces of evil in the heavenly realms* (Ephesians 6:12).

You've heard that Scriptures all your life. You've quoted it, but do you really believe it? You had better, if you are serious about seeing lasting freedom in your life. Paul also wrote, "So that we would not be outwitted by Satan; for we are not ignorant of his designs" (2 Corinthians 2:11, ESV). Did you know that Satan is using schemes and strategies against you? These strategies include unforgiveness, unresolved anger, rigid ungodly thinking, shame and more. Don't be ignorant of Satan's world system that is diametrically opposed to everything that's good and holy and beautiful in your life. He wants to destroy you and your relationships. Satan is out to steal, kill, and destroy you, but God wants you to have abundant life, and that includes abundant sexual life. (See John 10:10.)

The enemy is also a liar. He wants to oppress you and shame you for your sexual sins and make you feel too unworthy for God to turn your life around. He prosecutes and condemns you, and the sign of demonic oppression is when your mind is filled with condemning thoughts. The enemy reminds you of your sexual past and thereby shames and slanders you with unworthiness before the Lord.

Most of us can recognize this pattern. Sexual thoughts come into our minds, and we don't know where they came from. Standing and singing in the Sunday morning service, suddenly you have some memories of a past sexual sin arise in your mind tormentingly. Right in the middle of worship! Or you are out mowing the lawn when suddenly a whole new and original idea comes to your mind about how to orchestrate a sexual rendezvous with a certain woman. You are standing in a circle of friends at the campus ministry center when a particular young lady comes into the circle and greets a couple of people. As she walks away, you suddenly have a powerful sexual attraction to her, so strong that you internally berate yourself for your sinful passion.

All of these are real examples that have come to our attention through the Christian men that we have counseled. Temptation can come as a tidal wave in places that are seemingly safe. Even in church, the enemy knows us well enough to introduce temptation when our defenses may be down.

Again, we have a real enemy. We're not only fighting porn and our lust-wired brains! We are fighting an enemy who created this overwhelming pornographic culture of sexualized insanity, an enemy who wants to delude us, discourage us, destroy our sexual purity, and ultimately steal away our faith in God. He can kill the relational intimacy with both God and your wife, and he can destroy your confidence to pursue and enjoy the God-ordained privilege of sexual oneness with her. Remember, "The thief comes only to steal and kill and destroy" (John 10:10).

This is his scheme. He hates the godliness of sexual purity, and he's got a plan for corruption and ruin in the lives of men. In fact, he's probably more committed to his plan to destroy you than you are committed to a plan to stand against him. This is serious! "Be sober-minded; be watchful. Your adversary the devil prowls around like a roaring lion, seeking someone to devour. Resist him, firm in your faith" (1 Peter 5:8-9, ESV).

His plan includes exposing and taking advantage of your personal weaknesses. If you were abused as a child, Satan will take advantage of that situation to create in you a perverted view of sexuality. If you were scandalized in your heart at an early age by being exposed to something you were not mature enough to handle, then the enemy will take advantage of that to perpetuate the notion that shame and sex are always tied together. If you were emasculated as a young boy, then Satan will urge you to reaffirm your masculinity to yourself by overindulging in sexual escapades. If you were sexually promiscuous in high school, then he will shame you to secrecy; then when you mature to walk with Christ, the enemy will show up to torment you into believing that you will always be dirty and unacceptable to God.

These are only some of the ways he will ruin us. He will attempt to ruin us all, with schemes personally designed against us. Let us not be outwitted by Satan, for we are not ignorant of his schemes (see 2 Corinthians 2:11).

For many of us men this is not happening only in this one area. We have enough problems with our own histories, our own sexual sins, and the ways that we wired our brains. But on top of that, we have this enemy who knows how to make it *personal!* If we are ignorant, he will win. Let's not be outwitted. Let's not give him an advantage.

Being a disciple of Jesus Christ must include the spiritual skill set to manage this area of life. God has given us sex as a gift to enjoy. We older men would plead with you young men to learn the skills. Learn the grace-ways of walking in purity, so that you can enjoy the gift of your wife to the fullest.

"Naked and not ashamed!" Remember, that was the description of the Man and the Woman as they stood together in the Garden of Eden. The curse has stolen so much purity and beauty from us. But we can reclaim it. Let's take back any and all ground that Satan has taken from each of us individually. Through the purity in your heart, you can be intoxicated with the wife of your youth and embrace her in your arms in mutual delight and satisfaction.

ONE TACTIC, MANY WEAPONS

At the beginning of this chapter we quoted from one of the most beloved hymns of the history of the church, Martin Luther's great hymn, "A Mighty Fortress Is Our God." You hear that hymn in fewer places today as contemporary worship has replaced the hymnbook. But this old hymn contains a theological truth that reveals the way we are to handle the enemy. At the end of the third verse, Luther wrote: "One little word can fell him." One word will bring the enemy down. All we have to do is speak to the enemy, and tell him that we know the one word: *"Liar!"*

He's a liar. It's his nature to lie: "There is no truth in him. When he lies, he speaks his native language, for he is a liar and the father of lies" (John 8:44).

Satan has one tool. He lies.

But he does it in a thousand ways. With his lies, he can steal, kill, and destroy. In the realm of sex, he presents counterfeit delusions of sex appeal, false allures, seductions, deceit. In other words, lies.

You fight lies with the truth. In the kingdom of God, you fight lies with sound doctrine, with the two-edged sword of biblical truth. For the

Scriptures are the very breath of God: "All Scripture is breathed out by God and is profitable for teaching, for reproof, for correction, and for training in righteousness" (2 Timothy 3:16, ESV). When God speaks, His breath creates. When we speak His word, it creates faith in us. "So faith comes from hearing, and hearing through the word of Christ" (Romans 10:17, ESV).

When we are confronted with the lies of Satan, in faith we can call it for what it is. This requires us to be able to recognize a lie when we see or hear it! When Jesus was confronted with the temptations of Satan, our Lord simply quoted the Word of God. The Scriptures silenced the enemy and defeated him. The very words of the Bible rebuked him and stopped his lies. When Satan uses his tactics on us, by faith we can simply call him, "Liar!" and turn to speak scriptural truths from our hearts.

The battleground is the mind. This is the place where we must win the fight. This is where the battle turns in our favor.

A good tactic here is what we might call "Thought Stopping." When my mind is seduced to lust, leer, ogle, or fantasize, then I have to *stop* those thoughts. I have to *disrupt* them, and *turn* my mind to think instead on what is pure and godly. By faith, I can *interrupt* the lustful trajectory and replace those thoughts with truth.

When the enemy lures you into imagining something sexual, and most of the time it will be thoughts of another real woman, either from your past or present. Stop the thought! Interrupt the flow! Replace the defiling sexual fantasy with God-honoring words about the behavior, or even about the woman.

For example, let's say you find yourself worshiping in church, when suddenly you have a memory come to your mind, and it's the memory of your old girlfriend and your sexual excursions with her. Instead of going to shame and regret, insert your own thoughts that turn your mind back toward worship and thanksgiving. You could say something like this:

> Lord Jesus, I so regret my sins with _____, and how I
> defrauded her sexually. I thank you that in Christ I am forgiven.
> I pray for her today, and I pray that if she doesn't know you, you

will draw her to yourself on this Sunday morning, wherever she is. I pray that You will bless her and her marriage today. Thank you for the newness in my heart that you created when I came to know you. Thank you for my marriage. Lead me now in thankful worship before You.

When Satan reminds you of your sins, instead of going with him into shame and defeat, turn your thoughts to praise. When his thoughts come to your mind, turn them on him by saying:

Thank you, Liar, for bringing up my former sin; you just reminded me that I am forgiven. You just reminded me that Jesus Christ and I are one with each other. You just reminded me that I have been delivered from your old kingdom, which I used to live in. I have been *delivered from the domain of darkness and transferred to the kingdom of God's beloved Son, in whom I have redemption, the forgiveness of sins.* (see Colossians 1:13-14.) Thank you, Liar, for helping me to worship God today!

If he reminds you of your past, say, "Thank you, Liar, for reminding me that I am a forgiven and blessed child of God." Any brief "conversations" with the Liar should be finished by turning to a conversation with God. "Thank you, God, that You love me—always have and always will—and that You are conforming me to Your image in Christ."

If you wrestle with sexual thoughts about that woman on the other side of the church and you find yourself thinking, *Wow, look at that beautiful woman, wouldn't it be amazing to be with a woman like that?* then interrupt your thoughts and say:

That woman is not a sexual object to me. That's not who I am, for Christ has shared His life with me and that woman is a beautiful daughter of Our Father in Heaven. He is working His perfect will in her life, and mine as well, and that doesn't include those lustful thoughts.

If you are in the grocery store and you notice a beautiful woman in the produce section and the enemy's thought comes to your mind, "Wouldn't it be nice to be her husband?" Interrupt your internal words with something like this:

> Wow, Lord, she is attractive. You have made some very attractive women in this world, and sure enough there's one of them right there! Thank you that I am married to one of them, too. That woman reminds me that I am a sexual being, which is wonderful. Now I thank you for my beautiful wife at home. I'm going to praise my wife's beauty when I get home. I'm glad that I could serve her and our children by doing the grocery shopping today.

If you are a single man you could say:

> Wow, Lord, she is attractive. Thank you for making me a sexual being. I love it! One day I hope to be married to a woman that startles me with her beauty and allure every time I look at her, just as this woman has done to me. But today, I shall not dishonor myself or that woman over there by staring at her and fantasizing about her in my mind. **That's not who I am**. Instead, I will use this as an opportunity to prepare for my future marriage, and practice training my eyes to look away, and my heart to praise and thank You, and to keep on pushing my cart to the frozen food section to set my eyes on a beautiful carton of ice cream.

Stop the thoughts! Interrupt the pathway in your brain. Train yourself to speak the thoughts of God's Word, and rewire your mind to turn to beauty from lust.

Turn the tables on the Liar. Turn his accusations into thoughts of thankfulness and worship. Train your mind to interrupt, stop, and replace what entered your mind, training your mind to think on those things that are "pure, lovely, commendable, excellent, or worthy of praise" (see Philippians 4:8).

Train Satan, too. Train him to know that his tormenting schemes will not work against you, but that his schemes only will turn your mind to worship the Living God who loves you and has forgiven you! He doesn't want that, so train him to learn that you will always go to praise when he shows up.

Resist him and he will flee from you.

STRATEGY
Keep a picture of your wife in your wallet. When you need help directing your sexual drive toward intimacy with your wife, take a look at her beauty.

BREAKING SEXUAL BONDS WITH DOCTRINAL PRAYER

Some might say, "I've tried those techniques, and they work sometimes, but with certain women on certain days it doesn't work." Yes, we understand that. If the battle remains intense and the tormenting thought of a particular woman persists, then you can go to the next level of warfare.

We have counseled with many men who have had an affair and then come into our offices for help. After the affair is over and the man and his wife are recovering in therapy, the man will have a private conversation with us and say something like, "How do I get the other woman out of my mind? I constantly 'see' her. I have flashbacks in my mind to the images of her body! How do I get rid of these?"

Remember the power of our brains to record and store images. Our brains are very active during sex, as we have pointed out, creating memories of what we are seeing with our eyes, and literally bonding us to that woman. Anytime we have sex with a woman, you create a "oneness" with her chemically. You are bound to this woman physically, mentally and emotionally. You are one flesh with her.

The enemy can "trigger" your memories of the physical memory of being with a particular young lady. *Oh, wow, she was something!* You will be reminded of the pleasure and the arousal of your sexual sins with her, and the power of her image can trigger your regret and shame. These triggered thoughts will be like the "flaming darts of the evil one" (Ephesians 6:16, ESV). The "darts" are messages of guilty pleasure or shame that will enter your mind as you recall the images.

The following prayer is something I (Mark) recommend to men who are haunted by the sexual images of certain former sexual partners, regardless of whether you were single or married at the time. Since you have created a one-flesh relationship with her, every time you remember your sexual moments with that woman, you are burning the memory more strongly into your mind. This prayer can help with the breaking of the "oneness" and the cleansing of your soul, as well as with the rewiring of your brain and renewing of your mind:

Dear Heavenly Father,

I renounce the sexual use of my body with _____.

I renounce the "oneness" that was created with her and by doing this, I ask You to break all spiritual strongholds brought into my life through my involvement with her.

I renounce all alignmentI have given to any foothold I have given the enemy, and I break that alignment now, in Jesus' name.

I claim the forgiveness of Christ, the cleansing of His blood, and the renewal that comes with resurrection life.

I renounce the lies that I am unworthy and shameful because of these sins. As Christ accepts me, so I accept myself.

In the name of the Lord Jesus Christ, I here and now break every emotional, mental, relational, volitional, and spiritual stronghold that these sinful choices have made in my life. By the blood of the Lord Jesus, I take back all spiritual ground gained by the enemy, fill it with Yourself, and seal it off as holy ground.

Lord Jesus, I thank you that you have loved me and forgiven me through all of this.

I choose to forgive myself, too.

In Your name I pray. Amen.

IDENTITY: RECEIVE IT, BELIEVE IT, SPEAK IT

We fight the enemy's strategy by calling him a liar and by disrupting the thoughts that he spins our way. But another one of Satan's greatest strategies is identity theft. Satan steals your identity by reminding you of the pain and brokenness of your life, especially in the dimension of your sexual sins, and then he oppresses you into believing that your identity lies in the shadow of the shame of those memories.

To the contrary, by His grace God has granted you a new identity. He tells you that you are valuable, that He loves you, that you are acceptable to Him, and you are forgiven for all your sins. Satan comes to steal, kill, and destroy your confidence in that grace-based identity. When you medicate with self-sex, when you struggle with lust and pornography, then Satan shames you; he tells you that you are unworthy of God's love, that you are a complete disappointment to God. He steals your identity. "How could God love you, a man struggling with your sexual strongholds? You can't even quit! You are unworthy, and perhaps you are not even a Christian."

We have counseled with many men, especially young, single men in their teens and early twenties, who feel exactly this. In the aftermath of self-serving sexual sins, these young men feel so unworthy and faulty before God that some of them even doubt their salvation. Their sins convince them that they are unworthy of their identity in Christ.

A strong offense is the best defense against this attack from Satan. If he is going to try to talk us into an identity based on unworthiness or failure, then we will speak back to him the biblical power of our identity in Christ.

One of the best presentations of our identity in Christ is in the first chapter of the book of Ephesians. In verses 4 through 14 there are six characteristics listed referring to your new identity that is based on the grace of God:

(1) He *chose* you before He even created the heavens and the earth. (2) He joined Himself to you in spirit (see 1 Corinthians 6:17), so you are one spirit with Him. Thus, your spirit is *holy and blameless.* (3) Your Heavenly Father *adopted* you. You were adopted to reign in life (see Romans 5:17) with the Father. (4) You were *redeemed and forgiven* for all your sins, by the blood of the Lord Jesus. (5) You were *sealed in the Spirit,* guaranteeing that you belong to Him and that He will receive you to Himself as He promised.

What is your identity? You are a *chosen, holy and blameless, adopted, redeemed, forgiven, sealed-in-the-Spirit* child of God! That's who you are, whether you feel like it or not, whether you just looked at porn or not, whether you feel like a disappointment to God or not. You are a valuable treasure to Father, Son, and Holy Spirit. The Father chose you. The Son purchased you. The Spirit left Heaven to live in you. That makes you valuable. You are wanted. You are loved.

Receive this. Cry out for God to help you "see" this identity. Receive it. Believe it. Speak it. *The enemy has little chance to discourage or defeat a man who knows his identity in Christ.*

The next time the enemy douses cold water on your heart by shaming you for your failures, or fires a flaming missile into your mind to harass and oppress you by reminding you of past sexual sins or tempts you with new ones—Stop! The next time you look at yourself and despair that your heritage has robbed you of being strong and pure—Stop! When others speak words that condemn you and try to label you—Stop! Interrupt those thoughts. Go to scriptural truth. Start rewiring your brain with the truth, by declaring your identity, by speaking the truth about who the Word of God says you are. Receive it, believe it, and speak it:

I am a chosen, holy and blameless, adopted, redeemed, forgiven (forgiven!), sealed-in-the-Spirit child of God. That's who I am. Satan cannot take it away.

This identity has been granted to me freely by my relationship with the Father, the Son, and the Holy Spirit. My sins don't define me.

I don't listen to the voice of the enemy.

I agree only with the voice of my God and Savior.

Holy Spirit, open the eyes of my heart, and open my mouth to declare it.

I am accepted in Christ Jesus today!

INTIMACY: LOVE FOR GOD WILL CONQUER A THOUSAND SINS

What if you don't feel like standing? What if you don't feel like believing and speaking, and warring against the enemy? Do you ever have those days when you want to be a sexual daredevil (to use a figure of speech)? You know, those days when you are in the locker room with your buddies, and they are talking about a particular girl. You are getting lost in their comments, and you allow your imagination to paint a picture of what you are hearing about this girl. You enjoy the "feel good" of the dopamine in your body. At that moment, you don't want to "flee immorality" (see 1 Corinthians 6:18).

After having an argument with your wife, have you ever been angry, feeling unappreciated by her? You don't want to be pure in heart. You want to stay up late and look at porn, or you want to "take care of yourself," or you want to lie down in bed with your back to her and lustfully fantasize about an old girlfriend.

When I am weak, where can I find strength? What can help me now?

At that moment, there may not be much that can help you except to decide that you are going to love yourself enough to take care of yourself, and to not do anything stupid.

In the long run, there is no substitute for intimacy with God in the battle for sexual purity. Every man who wins this battle with sexual strongholds has somewhere in the journey been awakened to a powerful, new relationship of intimacy with the Father.

This is why we are here: to know God and enjoy Him forever. The purpose of God in our lives is not that we would learn some new, better, best behaviors, and rise up daily to be dutiful with the hope that our duties will keep us from sinning. That's just religion. No, the purpose of God in our lives is to have an intimate love relationship with us, through our new identity. God wants us to live and breathe in His love. "For the love of Christ controls us" (2 Corinthians 5:14, ESV). His love constrains us; it holds us together. It controls us in the battle for sexual purity. This intimacy will help us with the fight for freedom.

Until we learn how to relate with God, all other religious behaviors will do little for us. All the religious behaviors we try to adopt to keep our eyes from lusting, and to keep our heart from wandering will eventually fail. But "Love never fails" (1 Corinthians 13:8). Intimacy with God will conquer a thousand sins.

What produces intimacy?

Knowing someone. You cannot be intimate with someone you do not know. How do we get to know the Father, Son and Holy Spirit? We meet Him in His Word:

Those who worship Him must worship in spirit and truth (John 4:24, ESV).

Your word is truth (John 17:17).

Intimacy with God is based on meeting with Him in His Word, spirit to Spirit. We read. We receive. We read, again. He influences us to believe. We read and believe, and He renews our minds. We don't read it like the sports page, browsing for a few stats and highlights. We don't read it to gain some bit of knowledge, so we can nail our teenage son with it, or so we can posture over our wife with it. We read to receive. We read to be changed. We read to have our minds transformed into the image of Christ. We read so as to believe in the love of Father God. We read so as to receive the powerful influence of grace of the Lord Jesus. We read so as to be comforted and encouraged by the Holy Spirit. Spirit-taught truth will stand against the lies of the enemy, turning his temptations into empty exercises of futility. This is why Paul ended his second letter to the Corinthians this way: "The grace of the Lord Jesus, and the love of God and the fellowship of the Holy Spirit be with you all" (2 Corinthians 13:14).

To experience the intimacy of God it is imperative that you are able to hear His voice. If you can learn to hear Him speak to you through His Word, then your spirit will grow in the grace and power of His presence in your life. To experience His presence, we meet Him in His Word, but not with the typical way of reading. There is a method of meeting God in the Scriptures that we believe fosters a greater intimacy with Him, and it is a method not built around us studying the Word objectively, but built around a slower, more thoughtful way of listening and reading subjectively in prayer. We call it simply Reading with God.[49] We encourage you to discover the power of this ancient form of developing intimacy with God through praying and reading the Scriptures. So powerful is this ancient, monastic practice, that one church we know of has hundreds of men practicing the reading with God exercise daily. It has transformed the spiritual lives of these men, and is bringing a revolution to their men's ministry.

Give yourself to the practice of cleansing the heart and mind through the prayers of renunciation, through the believing and speaking of your identity in Christ, and through the powerful transformation of your heart in the reading with God exercise. This is spiritual warfare: to stand in the cleansing of the cross, in the power of your new identity, and in the intimacy of Spirit-taught truth. These are proven exercises that will grant a movement of God's love and grace on you and cause the rewiring of your brain. Stand in the love of the Father, in the grace of the Lord Jesus and in the fellowship of the Holy Spirit. Stand firm in intimacy with Him.

---

49 Reading with God is a sacred discipline of Scripture reading practiced in the sixth century in the monastery of Saint Benedict. The Latin name for this practice is *Lectio Divina*. For more information, see http://www.upwardcallministries.org/Scriptural_Reading_--_Lectio_Divina.pdf.

QUESTIONS FOR REFLECTION OR DISCUSSION

1. Pray these prayers and declare identity truths daily.

2. Practice the Reading with God on a regular basis. Take the time to practice it once a week, and then work your way up to twice a week, three times a week, etc.

3. Identify one accountability partner with whom you can agree to hold each other accountable to develop the discipline of these exercises. Agree to call each other every day to ask if you have done your meditation and prayed for one another.

14

HEALING YOUR MARRIAGE

Be kind to one another, tenderhearted, forgiving
one another, as God in Christ forgave you.
—EPHESIANS 4:32, ESV

Bill spent much of his childhood alone. His father worked for a large corporate lab as a chemist, and later head of a department that developed new pharmaceuticals. He was rarely at home, and when he was, he had little interest in spending time with his children. Bill and his two brothers felt a subtle jealousy from their father, who seemed to think that his own sons were in some way a threat to him as they became young men.

Bill's mother was an alcoholic, a lonely woman who sent strong messages that she was unloved by her husband and disinterested in her sons. Bill overheard her on more than one occasion say to a female friend on the phone, "I can't imagine ever really *liking* men." Bill wasn't sure why she held this opinion, but he knew that she did not express affection with comfort and ease like the moms on TV.

When he was a teenager, Bill's parents moved to a different school district, and in order to stay on the best football team in the state, he moved into a spare bedroom at his grandmother's house, which was a quiet haven. Grandma was a good cook who encouraged him to do his homework, and she loved to watch him play football.

At age 16, Bill was more handsome than most young men his age, and hours spent at the school gym, lifting weights and running around the football field, gave him a physique that was enviable. Before he knew what was happening, Bill had girls hanging all over him and competing for his attention. Some of them wanted more than that! And why not give in? If girls wanted to have sex with him—an activity he very quickly found to be highly enjoyable—then why not give them what they wanted?

When he was in college, he met Sharon, a girl who was perfect in every way—she was cute, fun, interested in him, and pure. She was just what he was looking for as a wife and mother of the family he wanted to have. For all of his machismo, Bill wanted what most men secretly want but don't talk about very much: people who loved him unconditionally and over the long run of life.

Bill married the princess of his dreams, and liked thinking of her as *his*. She was a faithful wife and a good mom. She was a willing sex partner, but Bill found that he had picked up a pattern of losing himself in online pornography and in meaningless encounters, which was a world of difference from what his wife longed for.

About this time, Bill learned that his father had kept a mistress for decades. The mistress, of course, was the reason for his mother's sadness. She was also the reason for his father's perception that his young, handsome, virile, athletic sons might be a threat.

If such a life was good enough for his father, Bill assumed it was good enough for him. He had his wife at home and on his arm for all respectable social and business events. He had his mistress available for fun.

However, Bill had been attracted to Sharon not only for her beauty, but her brains too. It didn't take long for her to recognize an unexplained hotel charge on the online bank statement or to note that Bill was constantly deleting his text message history. Before Sharon confronted Bill about his affair, he could not even picture his wife displaying emotions like anguish, fury, bitterness, and animosity. After he was caught and repented, Sharon started fighting a daily battle to show anything other than these emotions to Bill. What could he do?

SHOCK, ANGER, AND MORE

Men who increase their porn viewing nearly always become more self-centered, irritable, moody, and impatient. They seek out more distractions, spend less focused time with the family, and often become highly critical—including criticism of a wife's body and character. These patterns of behavior tend to escalate in frequency and potency over time.

A man who needs to confess sexual sins to his wife should not be at all surprised if his wife expresses extreme emotions when she discovers her husband's secretive behaviors, including shock, denial, anger, rage, depression, self-loathing, isolation, and fear. Virtually every woman experiences a degree of deep shame, embarrassment, and humiliation. Care must be taken to prepare the husband for making a disclosure and a wife for hearing it. If you have enlisted a pastor, Christian counselor, or wise accountability partner, consider talking through the disclosure with them in preparation.

Many therapists have noted that women who are betrayed by their husband's pornography use or affairs experience a range of symptoms that are usually associated with post-traumatic stress disorder. They feel powerless, have intrusive thoughts and memories, and they live with a deep sorrow and fear that something is going to remind them unexpectedly, day or night, of their husband's shameful behavior. They often become hyper-vigilant in checking computer histories, cell-phone records, and credit card receipts. Many become obsessive in seeking way to stop their husband's viewing of pornography or connection with another woman.

> **STRATEGY**
> If you have used pornography and your wife has discovered this, she may battle with negative self-esteem and insecurity. Go out of your way to give her at least one specific and genuine complement each day as you work to restore your relationship.

The stress a spouse feels over a husband's infidelity can produce sleepless nights, food issues (both under- and overeating), traumatic flashbacks, feelings of hopelessness, and crying spells. Once-healthy energetic women can express feelings of physical exhaustion in doing chores and fulfilling roles in the family that were once routine. Research show that even casual pornography usage lessens physical attraction to a spouse.[50] Intuitive wives can pick up on this change and their self-esteem can plummet.

Men should not be surprised when their wives display this wide range of emotions and responses. They need to "man up" to the truth: They not only need to seek healing for their own addiction, but they need to engage in serious damage control if they hope to heal their marriages.

BROKEN TRUST

Sexual sin of all kinds, especially a sexual affair, damages trust at an extremely deep level.

Trust is the most important ingredient in any relationship. It is also very fragile. Trust takes time to build, yet can be destroyed in an instant. Nevertheless, it is the glue that binds two people together in a meaningful connection.

---

50 Ana J. Bridges, "Pornography's Effect on Interpersonal Relationships," in *The Social Costs of Pornography: A Collection of Papers,* James R. Stoner and Donna Hughes (eds.) (Princeton, N.J.: Witherspoon Institute, 2010), 89-110.

Trust is always a two-way street. It involves being vulnerable one to another.

How do you begin to rebuild trust when a relationship has been broken?

First, recognize that the trust was destroyed because of *sin*. If the one who broke the trust confesses that sin and experiences God's forgiveness, and if the person truly seeks to repent and lead a new life, then the relationship has a *chance* of being reconciled.

Second, the one who has been hurt, and who believes trust has been violated, must make a willful *decision* to forgive.

Forgiveness is not a feeling; it is an act of the *will*. Forgiveness does not mean that the offense didn't happen. Neither does it mean that there was no pain. Nor does it mean that the person cannot be held accountable for negative consequences associated with the offense. To forgive means that the person who has been hurt "releases" the offender into the hands of God and leaves all chastisement and justice to God, knowing fully that God not only is willing to accept that responsibility, but that God has ways and means of establishing lasting justice that a hurting person cannot know.

As part of the forgiveness process, the offender also needs to forgive *himself.* And in most cases, he needs to ask for forgiveness from his spouse or others he has hurt by his sin.

Forgiveness is the cornerstone for the rebuilding of a relationship.

Trust is always earned. If trust has been violated, it takes time for the "earning of new trust" to develop. Tremendous patience is sometimes required, and new patterns of behavior must be in full evidence for trust to begin to be restored.

How can you tell if you are *not* trusting another person? There is a constant and nagging feeling of suspicion and unrest. A lack of trust often manifests as frustration, placing of demands, running away, self-pity, anger, and even frenetic behavior. If a person feels that sex is manipulative, trust is usually absent.

> **STRATEGY**
> If you have fallen into a pattern of using your wife for sexual release instead of engaging in true intimacy, challenge yourself to focus on non-sexual touch and verbal affirmation of your wife. Some may choose to consider this a season of prayer and/or fasting (see 1 Corinthians 7:5) and wait until their wife initiates sex.

Forgiveness requires intention—it doesn't happen without a willful *granting* of forgiveness. It takes courage. In many cases, it is easier for the spouse of the offender to walk away than to do the difficult work of rebuilding a marriage. The offender needs to acknowledge the courage of his wife if she chooses to remain in relationship with him.

And finally, forgiveness is not a one-time event. A person may need to forgive repeatedly—any time there is a wounding memory or a relapse, any time there is an example of rejection or anger. Knowing that the process of forgiveness is just that—a *process*—is often very helpful, but the process should never be used as an excuse or justification for resorting to addictive fantasies or behaviors. The offender bears the bulk of responsibility for *winning* the trust of his spouse.

Consider this metaphor. If a woman is a passenger in a car driven by her out-of-control husband and he steers their car into a tree, she is not going to be eager to get back in that car with him without some sort of reassurance that he'll drive more safely. And even if he takes driver safety classes and pays fines, she is still going to struggle. She is likely to look diligently for signs that he will protect her, and she will deeply resent any suggestion on his part that she "just trust him." In some cases, the woman is going to feel safe only if *she* is driving the vehicle—and in terms of a marriage, she may become much more assertive in demanding what she needs, and the boundaries that she requires for the marriage to continue. Over time, though, if the husband continually chooses to drive safely—especially when she is riding with him—the wife may come to trust him again.

Men tend to resent this, of course, but the truth is—he is going to face consequences for his behavior, and rebuilding trust with a spouse is one of those challenges.

HELPING A SPOUSE GET HELP

After a man admits to sexual sin, he is often at a loss as to *how* to help his wife, but he needs to support her in getting help should she need it.[51]

First and foremost, she needs a safe place to be "heard" and to voice her pain and feelings of loss, shame, and confusion.

The spouse needs appropriate disclosure from her husband as trust gets rebuilt.

She needs affirmation that she didn't cause his battle, can't control it, and can't cure it.

The wife of a man battling sexual sin who is seeking healing needs her own counseling to help her heal from the trauma of her husband's behavior. She especially needs:

1. *Physical self-care.* She needs to learn how to handle her own increased stress, and actively seek healing—often, this means more sleep, a healthier diet, exercise, stretching, long soaking baths, quiet times for prayer and contemplation, and shedding unnecessary responsibilities and obligations in order to have more time for self, and more interaction with her children.

2. *Spiritual grounding.* A woman who experiences betrayal by her husband's sexual battle needs the comfort that comes through prayer and reading God's Word. She needs time

---

51 Mark's wife Debbie has written a wonderful book on healing for betrayed spouses, *Shattered Vows* (Grand Rapids, MI: Zondervan, 2008).

and opportunity to heal *spiritually*. Not all women are eager to reach out to close friends or people in her church—many feel false guilt or shame for what their husbands have done and they are often very vulnerable in admitting these feelings. An objective Christian therapist is often the best resort.

3. *Simplifying life.* She needs to be able to maintain a simple structure for her life, with as much predictability as possible. A frenzied pace with too many commitments can only increase her feelings of exhaustion, and lead to more intense feelings of hopelessness, failure, powerlessness, and futility. A woman is wise to slow down, reevaluate her priorities, and say "no" to anything that is not absolutely essential.

4. *Expressing emotions.* A woman may find it helpful to write her feelings in a new journal that she knows "going in" she may throw away at a later date. She needs to give herself full permission to write about her most intense, raw feelings. She may find that this journal is helpful if she seeks out a professional counselor. It can serve as a starting point for conversations. She must not be critical of her own emotions. She must *choose not to live in an ongoing state of denial, anger, or bitterness.* Emotions, once expressed, need to be brought to a point of being able to forgive—not only forgiving her spouse, but forgiving *herself* for whatever she may be blaming herself.

MARRIAGE COUNSELING

These men and their wives need to get marriage counseling, together, in a therapeutic setting. The man may need special counseling on how to be a better husband, the woman may need counseling on how to be a better wife, but the main focus needs to be on how the two can build a new and better relationship. They both need to revisit God's plan for marriage.

From the beginning, according to the Bible, God's plan for sex and marriage were related and exclusive. Sex was to occur between one man and one woman in a relationship that had an overarching theme of "oneness." Oneness included a strong spiritual, emotional, and relational bonding that was enhanced by the sexual union of intercourse, but not created solely by it. The best sex has always been sex in which two people are deeply and intimately joined in heart and mind.

God said to Adam and Eve: "A man shall leave his father and his mother and hold fast to his wife, and they shall become one flesh" (Genesis 2:24-25, ESV). Some men need to learn how to "leave and cleave." Some women also.

At times, couples benefit from rekindling a practice of dating (date night) and even courting, as they seek to renew their marriage. And in some cases, there can be wonderful benefit in having a "renewal of marriage vows" ceremony to mark a transition from the old pain into the new hopes and dreams.

Some of the best marriages we know have walked this painful road.

STRATEGY

There are strong resources out there to help you restore and improve your relationship with your wife. Try doing a 40-day "love dare." (Visit http://www.40daylovedare.com/.)

THE "FOUR TS"

Remember Bill and Sharon from earlier in this chapter? Some time has passed, and now Bill and Sharon are involved in what Bill describes as "a great love story." To watch the ease with which Sharon slips her hand into Bill's at church or the frequent laughter that bubbles up in their conversations, you would have a hard time imagining that they had ever faced hardship.

How in the world did they get back to intimacy? Bill was battling such a stronghold, and Sharon had such a battle with bitterness and anger.

Thankfully, Bill saw a Christian counselor who not only helped Bill use Scripture and accountability to fight against his shame and strongholds, but also introduced Bill and Sharon to the "four Ts" of marital intimacy:[52]

Time—African writer Ernestine Banyolak beautifully illustrates the concept of lovemaking. "A man's experience is like a fire of dry leaves. It is easily kindled, flaring up suddenly and dying down just as quickly. A woman's experience on the other hand is like a fire glowing charcoal. Her husband has to tend to these coals with loving patience. Once the blaze is burning brightly, it will keep on glowing and radiating warmth for a long time". Take time for love and each other.

Bill and Sharon are committed and connected, but this restoration of intimacy, an even deeper intimacy than they had experienced early on in marriage, did not come overnight. Bill and Sharon poured hours into reading Scripture, meditating on God's word, journaling, spending time together, and attending joint and individual sessions with a Christian counselor. The process took time.

Talk—Partners who experience great intimacy are able to share meaningful parts of their life with the one they love. Communication precedes sexual intimacy. Good sex is the fruit of caring for, accepting, and valuing your love before, during and after lovemaking. Many couples I have worked with lost their habits of checking in with each other daily from work or engaging in "pillow talk" after sex.

Bill did not even realize that, as much as he loved Sharon, he had walls up that impeded his communication with her. Bill used to think that he just didn't enjoy long conversations, but he has come to learn that before he just did not know how to do intimacy, and he was uncomfortable

---

52 See the article by Tim Clinton, "Is porn good for your marriage?" at http://timclinton.com/articles/45/is-porn-good-for-your-marriage/.

letting his walls down. Now that the habit of communication has become more regular, Bill looks forward to talking with Sharon, and it has become his favorite part of each day.

Touch—We have lost the art of touch. Secure lovers are able to participate in meaningful non-sexual touch. Back rubs, holding hands, a gentle kiss, holding each other, a stroke of the hair. Such meaningful touch is a gateway to bonding emotionally, relationally, and physically. These acts, if remembered often, will only serve to draw you closer and enhance intimacy.

Under the suggestion of their counselor, Bill and Sharon stopped having sex for a period of a few weeks. They worked on greeting each other with a kiss when Bill returned from work and showing non-sexual affection. The agreement was that Bill and Sharon would abstain from sex for a time until Sharon felt her desire for intimacy with Bill return. A large part of what helped Sharon rebuild this desire was the nonsexual touch that was slowly worked back into the relationship. While Bill was not excited about a sexual hiatus when the plan was made, he experienced a new joy and thrill when Sharon began to again initiate sex with Bill.

Tenderness—Noted author Ingrid Trobisch wrote, "the greatest erogenous zone in a woman's body is her heart." Sex was never meant to be a single act of expression or feeling. On the contrary, gentleness, acts of kindness, and self-sacrifice, those little words that fit in the little big word "love" all combine to become the building blocks of sexual satisfaction. Sex is about joining with your partner as God designed for warmth, intimacy, and bonding.

Bill began weaving intentional kindness and uplifting encouragement into his daily interactions with his wife. While he was not mean or rude in his first years with Sharon, he was also not intentionally tender with her. As Bill began to practice tenderness, he began to feel more tender emotions toward his wife. Sharon's response to Bill's tenderness strengthened their bond and satisfaction with the relationship.

Proverbs 5:15-19 describes a joyful, intimate relationship between a man and his wife:

Drink water from your own cistern, running water from your own well. Should your springs overflow in the streets, your streams of water in the public squares? Let them be yours alone, never to be shared with strangers. May your fountain be blessed, and may you rejoice in the wife of your youth. A loving doe, a graceful deer—may her breasts satisfy you always, may you ever be intoxicated with her love.

The new "marriage" can be better than the old—that's a hope both spouses can embrace fully.

QUESTIONS FOR REFLECTION OR DISCUSSION

1. Is there an unconfessed sexual sin putting a wall up between you and your spouse? How can you be wise and humble in confession? Consider writing your thoughts out in a letter or seeking specific guidance on your specific situation from a trusted mentor.

2. Has a lack of trust impacted your relationship? What has that looked like in your day-to-day life?

3. What are your hopes and dreams for true intimacy with your spouse?

ACTION ITEMS

1. Determine if marriage counseling is needed and seek a trusted Christian resource through your church or a clinic. If you do not feel that counseling is needed, make sure your spouse and potentially a mentor are in agreement.

2. Plan some specific time through a retreat, a weekend away, or more frequent date nights to focus on building your relationship with your spouse.

15

FIGHTING FOR A LEGACY: PASSING FREEDOM TO THE NEXT GENERATIONS

*For this is the will of God, that you
abstain from sexual immorality.*
—1 THESSALONIANS 4:3, ESV

*Fight for your families, your sons and your
daughters, your wives and your homes.*
—NEHEMIAH 4:14

There is a man in the Old Testament with the character of a warrior. His name was Nehemiah and he stood his ground on the wall. He did not let the fear of a battle drive him away from his calling. He prayed for God's protection, and then he prepared for imminent attack from an enemy he did not take lightly. Nehemiah had a wise strategy:

Prepare when you are strong for a time when you will be weak.

Nehemiah wasn't an intimidating figure nor was he necessarily a man of physical strength, but he was a leader with a courageous heart. God had an assignment for him that was a huge and dangerous task that required unusual people skills. His enemies tried to lure him off this assignment, but he stayed true to the task, and was found faithful to the end. He was sent by God around the middle of the fourth century B.C. to rebuild the walls of Jerusalem.

The walls had been knocked down and the gates had been burned more than a hundred years earlier by the Babylonian siege against the city. As the repair work began, we read of two regional enemies of the Jews who became furiously angry, and began to plot as to how they might stop the work on the wall. In the fourth chapter of the book of Nehemiah these men are mentioned by name, Sanballat and Tobiah. Their tribal forefathers had once lived under the dominion of Judah's former kings, so they did not want Nehemiah to succeed.

When Sanballat and Tobiah threatened a fight to disrupt the work, Nehemiah caught wind of their plans. His first response was to pray to God for His protection, and then encourage the people to not be afraid. Then he divided his workforce into two shifts. He had half of the work crew keep on working, while the other half stood guard with their swords, spears and bows. In the weakest and lowest places of the wall, he stationed whole families to stand together.

At the time of strength, Nehemiah kept the wall building on pace, but he also bulked up for a war. He strengthened his fortifications during a time of peace, so that at the time of attack, his people were not vulnerable. When the enemies backed off from the fight, Nehemiah sent everyone back to work. But even then, those who could manage it used one hand to carry building materials and the other hand to carry a weapon. To combat their fear, Nehemiah told them, "Don't be afraid of them. Remember the Lord, who is great and awesome, and fight for your families, your sons and your daughters, your wives and your homes" (Nehemiah 4:14).

The walls of Jerusalem were very important to the people of Israel; their songs and poems spoke of the walls as the symbol of strength and security. In Psalm 51, David's famous psalm of repentance for his adultery with Bathsheba, he concluded with a plea for God to use him to strengthen the other men of Israel in the battle for sexual purity. In the final verses of that psalm, David referred to this work of God on our hearts as the "building of the walls of Jerusalem" (see Psalm 51:18).

This is our calling from God, too. Nehemiah was called to rebuild the literal walls of Jerusalem. Like David, we are called to rebuild the spiritual walls of His kingdom, and those walls are our hearts! Fight for your heart, and you will be fighting for your wives and your sons and daughters. Fight for your heart, and then fight for your brothers on the wall.

We have a calling from God: Stay on the wall! We must allow the grace and life of the Lord Jesus Christ to be formed in our hearts. He is our life, and He is sexually pure. Therefore, as new creations, we too are pure in spirit, in our oneness with Him. We must not let our enemies defeat us and trap us in sexual sin, so that we betray our true selves in Christ Jesus. We must stay on the wall!

- We are called to be men of passion and purity.

- We are called to be righteous as fathers and husbands.

- We are called to the integrity of our vocations and ministries.

- We are called to build the integrity of our own hearts.

The integrity of this wall, the wall of righteousness in our hearts, will determine whether we stand or fall in the time of the battle.

For, like Nehemiah, we have enemies, too. One of them hates the wall, and doesn't want it to be raised. He wants to get us off the wall, and draw us into a battle away from the wall, where he knows that we will fall. Every temptation from him is to get us off the wall and fall into sexual sin. For he knows the power of sexual sin, which is like no other sin in the damage that it can do to us on the inside (see 1 Corinthians 6:18).

Knowing this, the enemy would relish the opportunity to deceive us. We are just one click away, just one kiss away, from the devastation that this sin can rain in our hearts.

God has let it be known that our legacy can last for generations:

You shall not bow down to them or serve them, for I the Lord your God am a jealous God, visiting the iniquity of the fathers on the children to the third and the fourth generation of those who hate me, but showing steadfast love to thousands of those who love me and keep my commandments (Exodus 20:5-6, ESV).

Do you see, men, how long your sin can influence your family? Without the intervention of Christ and His grace, sin can have a legacy of four generations! However, that also means there is an exponential miracle in faithfulness. Winning the fight of your life can leave a legacy for thousands. Faithfulness can generate the miraculous!

STRATEGY
When you have small victories in your battle,
take time to enjoy the feeling of accomplishment.
Thank God for giving you the strength to overcome,
and commit the positive emotions to memory.
Recall the victory when you feel tempted later.

WHERE SIN ABOUNDS, GRACE ABOUNDS EVEN MORE

Dear Men, let us remind you of the brute realities that have been highlighted in this book. Single, young men, be sober-minded. Your problems with lust and desire will not go away with marriage. Married men, you now know why it has never gone away. You have wired your brains with years of lust, pornography, self-satisfaction, and more. Marriage does not automatically change your brain. You only change your brain by the renewing of your mind, your emotions, and your behaviors. You must understand your story and be accountable to healthy-minded men, living in the forgiveness and grace of God.

Don't be discouraged by this next statement, for it is true for every sin we struggle with in the church. *There is no final victory while living in the flesh.* This is a battle where you must keep winning, and keep standing in the ground you have won. Don't get a measure and a season of freedom and run around claiming that you have won the victory and your fight is over. Only a narcissist is that delusional.

Your legacy is to be a warrior, and to teach your sons to be warriors. You will have seasons of freedom. You might have years of purity and strength, where the temptation seems gone forever. But temptation can come back fiercely one day. Even men from older generations struggle with porn and lust—it is not only a struggle for youth. In a recent nationwide survey, half of men age 50-68 admitted to looking at porn monthly or more![53]

When David committed adultery with Bathsheba, he was a mature man of God. He had won many battles, and his victory over Goliath had been long ago. But when he fell into this sin, David found a deeper spiritual intimacy with God afterward. Psalm 51 teaches the same principle that Paul teaches in Romans: *Where sin abounds, grace abounds all the more.* God will meet you in your broken places, and from that place of brokenness His life can flow, if you receive His recreating work in your heart. David asked God to create in him a clean heart and a steadfast faithfulness (see verse 10), and to restore the joy of intimacy with Him (see verse 12).

Then, David said something to God that becomes our ultimate challenge to you men, too. We end this part of our journey here, with this: *It's not just about you.* It's about receiving the restoration work of God in your heart, so that you can share it with others. Just as sexual sin can affect many areas of your life and impact those around you—your victory can

---

53 Proven Men Ministries (http://www.provenmen.org/2014pornsurvey/pornography-use-and
-addiction/).

do the same. There is power to declare God's victory over sin not only at the cross, but as a redemptive restored life. David promised God, "Then I will teach transgressors your ways, so that sinners will turn back to you" (Psalm 51:13).

God's plan is to do His powerful purifying work in your heart, so that you can learn His ways. Then you can turn to other men around you, to your sons standing nearby, and you can teach them the way of God's deliverance from sexual strongholds. Show them that even though it is difficult, it is possible.

Men, we need such warriors. We need men who will fight off the enemy and rebuild their spiritual walls. We need men who can find the way to living pure and strong in the heart. The men of the church are struggling in silence. They feel that they are all alone, and they hear of precious few men who are walking in the power of freedom. The church desperately needs men who know the way out. We need you to get free. As each one of us can find the way out, then we can help the rest of the men imprisoned, sitting in the pews.

Someone in your home, someone in your church, someone in your men's group must find the way out, or we will all remain shackled and defeated by sexual sins! One man must break the slavery to this enemy. One man must find God's way of controlling mind and body, and controlling the sexual arena. Then this man can teach the men around him, and we can raise up an army of strong warriors, who are leading our families and churches to freedom.

We need you to join us in the fight of your life.

Never give up!

Never give up. God is still working. Your frustration and crying out is a gift from God in you. Consider the alternative, if you don't fight. The most profound act of God might not be the quick deliverance you are hoping for, but it will be His granting you the grace to keep standing in the fight. Don't let momentary failure be your final defeat, men. Remember: "Where sin increases, grace abounds all the more" (see Romans 5:20).

Don't surrender. Stay in the fight. Grace is abundant and free.

The enemy has not given up. He did not quit and go home.

Remember the end game, down here on planet Earth: to be ravished in her love! Not just to make love to your wife, but to experience *oneness* as God intended. That's the reward that God has laid out before us. Don't ever lose sight of that.

CHARLIE'S LEGACY: WORTH IT ALL!

Charlie had to resign from pastoring a large church because of sexual strongholds in his life. He stepped down, with his marriage and family hanging by a thread, and went into counseling to understand his story, and why this stronghold had such a grip on him. He met with a counselor early on who gave him a psychological test, and when the counselor read him the results, he said, "Charlie, according to your profile, you are one of those who will quit counseling early. You need to know that if you try to go back into a church ministry, I feel it will be my duty before God to call the leaders of that church and tell them you are not safe, that you are not ready."

Such boldness and bluntness added to Charlie's brokenness before God. At first, he felt trapped. He felt powerless. He felt that God had hemmed him in. Charlie told us that he felt he had only two options. One, just commit suicide and leave his wife to be known as the widow instead of the poor, pitiful wife of that failed pastor. Or two, start walking, one day at a time, meeting weekly with his counselor, and giving God the benefit of the doubt; see if God might heal him, heal his marriage, and maybe one day, restore some kind of a ministry.

While Charlie thought about his two options, he started walking a day at a time. He kept walking right into option two. Six years of counseling, never quitting. In the back of his mind were those words, "your profile shows that you will quit counseling early." Charlie determined to not quit or let the odds define him. He determined to outlast everyone!

He kept walking. God kept working. He outlasted everyone but God. Friends left him. Fellow pastors in his city abandoned him. But God healed his wife, and she lasted, too. Charlie walked into maturity, and found the freedom he had longed for.

Many years later, at an engagement party for his grown daughter, Charlie had a unique moment with friends and family to share more personally the details of his journey. One person was not there to hear it, his soon to be son-in-law, Kevin, who was running late to the gathering, and missed the telling of the story. After telling it, his daughter came up to him quietly and said, "I want you to tell your story to Kevin when he gets here. I want him to know how hard you've worked."

Charlie's heart broke under the grace of God. Oh, what a gift from his daughter! He *had* walked. God *had* worked. It took years of submitting to the journey to which God had called him. But now Charlie understood his story. He saw the loneliness in his early life, and he saw the foolish, rebellious ways he had tried to heal that loneliness through sexual misdeeds. He understood every lie of the stronghold thinking that had kept him trapped. He had replaced those lies, and learned to rewire his brain with the truths that would set him on a course toward freedom.

But the greatest reward was that his daughter saw it too, and she spoke it. That was the crowning reward from God. His own daughter received the legacy of Charlie's hard work, his faith-walk of trust in the grace of God.

Invest in the fight of your life, men. Receive the crowning reward from your children. Let them know that you have fought this fight, and that you are fighting this fight with other men. Don't hide it from them.

We must stand! We must fight this fight of grace! We must build the walls of our heart, fortify that wall, and strengthen its integrity. By grace through faith, we can stand. We can reign in the fight of our lives. Then, one day our children and grandchildren will rise up and say, "I am blessed by God, for I have a father who stands and reigns in life. He is winning in the fight of our lives!"

A FINAL ACTION STEP

Write a vision statement about becoming the man God called you to be. Consider the legacy that you want to leave your children and others as you write this statement. Print this up and keep it before you. Finally, tell it to as many people as you can. For those of you not married, keep this vision of the commitment you make to any potential marriage partner. For those of you who are married, share it with your wife.

16

YOUR HALFTIME SPEECH: LIVING THE DREAM (TO LOVE AND BE LOVED)

My beloved is mine and I am his.
—SONG OF SOLOMON 2:16

Billy Sunday, the great prohibitionist, fought a battle against alcoholism, but it is said that he died wih the taste of alcohol on his lips.

It's a battle to break free. Once you have tasted freedom, enjoy it to its fullest, protecting yourself from ever going back to bondage. Hebrews 12:1 says "Therefore, since we are surrounded by so great a cloud of witnesses, let us also lay aside every weight, and sin which clings so closely, and let us run with endurance the race that is set before us" (ESV).

Own your issue. Square up to that sin and take it head-on. Fight the good fight.

We are more than conquerors through Him who loves us. See yourself there and never look back.

When you have moved to a place of freedom in your life, that means you have been honest with yourself about your journey. You know what your triggers are and have the insight to make deliberate choices that insulate you from the temptations.

Freedom means you will have made a covenant with God that the eyes of your heart will not defile God's daughters. You will see them in the beauty of who they are, looking them in the eyes, free from lust and shame. Freedom means you love and are able to be loved—with God and those closest to you.

What will it look like in your marriage? Perhaps similar to these words from Song of Solomon:

> *Like a lily among the thorns, so is my darling among the maidens. Like an apple tree among the trees of the forest, so is my beloved among the young men. In his shade I took great delight and sat down, and his fruit was sweet to my taste* (Song of Solomon 2:2-3, NASB).

You'll enjoy time together. There will be pillow talk, and there will be tenderness in your touch. You will connect and disclose your dreams, failures, goals, aspirations, and more.

And the sex will be deeper and more fulfilling. You will be able to participate, fully present, in the moment, in a meaningful way, with eyes wide open.

Picture yourself able to deal with the burn in your soul—with your wife as the object of your desire. It takes honor. It takes the hard work of making yourself a safe person who gets her. But consider the reward.

Finally, we want all of you to know that we (Tim and Mark) as men, husbands, fathers, counselors, and teachers will pray daily for all of you men. We trust that you have been blessed, encouraged, challenged, and strengthened by this book. We join together now in the name of Jesus Christ and in the power of the Holy Spirit. We are God's team.

It's game time. **Let's roll.**

Appendix

SEXUAL INTEGRITY INVENTORY

Please answer the following questions by circling the appropriate response. You will be given directions on scoring at the end of the Inventory.

1. Have you ever tried to stop a certain type of sexual behavior without long-term success?

    ☐ Yes ☐ No

2. Do you regret the amount of time you spend online in online sexual chats, viewing porn, webcam sex, chatting with prostitutes, etc.?

    ☐ Yes ☐ No

3. Would it be true to say that your parents never talked to you in a helpful way about sex?

    ☐ Yes ☐ No

4. Do you feel preoccupied or distracted by your sexual thoughts or activity?

    ☐ Yes ☐ No

5. Have you on multiple occasions kept hidden from or lied to some-one you loved about using pornography?

☐ Yes ☐ No

6. Do your wife, friends, or family ever worry or complain about your sexual behavior?

☐ Yes ☐ No

7. Has your involvement with porn, online hook-ups, sex and dating websites, cruising social networks for sex, etc., become greater than your intimate contacts with your wife?

☐ Yes ☐ No

8. Were you ever sexually abused by anyone in your young life?

☐ Yes ☐ No

9. In the last week have you looked at pornography?

☐ Yes ☐ No

10. Have you ever engaged in looking at pornography or masturbating daily, including your adolescent or teenage years?

☐ Yes ☐ No

11. Have you ever thought that a sexual activity you have engaged in is totally "weird"?

☐ Yes ☐ No

12. Do you look forward to family events being over or for a spouse or significant other to go someplace without you so you can more easily engage in sexual activity?

☐ Yes ☐ No

13. Have you had certain kinds of sex or had sex with certain people that later disgusted you when you thought back on it?

☐ Yes ☐ No

14. Do you believe that sexual activity has kept you from having more long-term intimate relationships or from reaching other personal goals?

    ☐ Yes ☐ No

15. Have you ever felt bored with sex in your marriage?

    ☐ Yes ☐ No

16. Do you expect your wife to submit to your sexual requests all or most of the time?

    ☐ Yes ☐ No

17. Have you ever become angry with your wife for saying no?

    ☐ Yes ☐ No

18. Do you often find that you would rather look at pornography or masturbate than have sex with your wife?

    ☐ Yes ☐ No

19. Does your wife ever complain that you are not attracted to her or that you have little sexual interest in her?

    ☐ Yes ☐ No

20. Does your wife ever complain about your sexual demands?

    ☐ Yes ☐ No

21. Have you ever had an affair?

    ☐ Yes ☐ No

22. Have you had more than one affair?

    ☐ Yes ☐ No

23. Do you ever use masturbation to manage stress or to go to sleep?

    ☐ Yes ☐ No

24. Have you ever used masturbation to avoid pressuring your wife for sex?

    ☐ Yes ☐ No

25. Have you ever lost a job because of looking at porn while at work or because you had sex or an affair with a co-worker?

    ☐ Yes ☐ No

26. Do your sexual activities ever place you in danger of arrest or have you ever been arrested?

    ☐ Yes ☐ No

27. Have you ever potentially exposed a loved one or spouse to a sexually transmitted disease and not told them about it?

    ☐ Yes ☐ No

28. Has anyone ever been hurt emotionally by events related to your sexual behavior (e.g., lying to your partner or friends, or not showing up for event/appointment due to sexual activity)?

    ☐ Yes ☐ No

29. Have you ever been sexual with a minor, or when you were a minor, did you ever have sex with someone much younger than you?

    ☐ Yes ☐ No

30. When you have sex, do you feel depressed afterwards or later regret it?

    ☐ Yes ☐ No

31. Have you made repeated promises to yourself or another person to change some form of your sexual activity only to break them later?

    ☐ Yes ☐ No

32. Have you ever wondered about your sexual preferences?

    ☐ Yes ☐ No

33. Have your sexual activities interfered with some aspect of your professional or personal life (e.g., caused problems at work, loss of relationship)?

    ☐ Yes ☐ No

34. Have you ever feared being homosexual?

    ☐ Yes ☐ No

35. Have you engaged in repeated experiences of unsafe or "risky" sex even though you knew it could cause you harm?

    ☐ Yes ☐ No

36. Have you had more than one sexually transmitted disease?

    ☐ Yes ☐ No

37. Have you ever had sex with someone just because you were feeling aroused and later felt ashamed or regretted it?

    ☐ Yes ☐ No

38. Have you ever cruised public restrooms, rest areas, gym locker rooms and/or other public places seeking anonymous sexual encounters with strangers?

    ☐ Yes ☐ No

39. Have you ever talked to a pastor or professional counselor, psychologist, or doctor about your sexual behaviors?

    ☐ Yes ☐ No

40. Did you think that marriage would solve your sexual problems with lust and fantas,y and were disappointed when they didn't?

    ☐ Yes ☐ No

    Total Number of Yes Answers: _____

Scoring: If you answered yes to half or more of these questions, you may struggle with addiction, chronic infidelity, or shame about your sexual history. Please talk to a pastor or professional counselor. Please feel free to contact our office or go to our website, www.faithfulandtrue.com, for more information.

Disclaimer: This assessment is for informational purposes only and cannot substitute for a full evaluation by a clinical professional; the inventory should only be used as a guide to understanding your sexual behavior and the potential consequences associated with that behavior.

RESOURCES

WEBSITES

The American Association of Christian Counselors: www.aacc.net

Faithful and True: www.faithfulandtrue.com

L.I.F.E. Recovery International: www.freedomeveryday.org

Porn to Purity Ministries: www.porntopurity.com

The Pure Life Alliance: www.purelifealliance.org

Freedom Begins Here: www.freedombeginshere.org

The Purity Network: www.puritynetwork.info

One Million Men Porn Free: www.join1millionmen.org

BIBLIOGRAPHY

Additional Books by Mark and Debbie Laaser

Carnes, Patrick. Laaser, Debra, and Laaser, Mark. (1999). *Open Hearts: Renewing Relationships with Recovery, Romance and Reality.* Wickenburg, AZ: Gentle Path Press. ISBN 1-929866-00-3.

Haas, Melissa. (2005). *A L.I.F.E. Guide: Spouses Living in Freedom Everyday.* Grand Rapids, MI: Color House Graphics. ISBN 0-9771662-1-X.

Laaser, Debra. (2008). *Shattered Vows.* Grand Rapids, MI: Zondervan. ISBN 978-0-310-27394-3.

Laaser, Mark. (1992). *Healing the Wounds of Sexual Addiction*. Grand Rapids, MI: Zondervan. ISBN 0-310-25657-7 (formerly *Faithful and True*).

___. (1999). *Talking to Your Kids About Sex*. Colorado Springs, CO: WaterBrook Press. ISBN 1-57856-199-X.

___. (2002). *A L.I.F.E. Guide: Men Living in Freedom Everyday*. Fairfax, VA: Xulon Press. ISBN 1-591602-53-X.

___. (2011). *Becoming a Man of Valor*. Kansas City, MO: Beacon Hill Press. ISBN 978-0-8341-2740-1.

___. (2011). *The Seven Principles of Highly Accountable Men*. Kansas City, MO: Beacon Hill Press, 2011. ISBN 978-0-8341-2742-5.

___. (2011). *Taking Every Thought Captive*. Kansas City, MO: Beacon Hill Press. ISBN 978-0-8341-2741-8.

___. (2015). *Faithful and True Workbook*. Eden Prairie, MN: Faithful and True, Inc. ISBN 0-8054-9819-2.

Laaser, Mark and Debra. (2008). *The Seven Desires of Every Heart*. Grand Rapids, MI: Zondervan. ISBN 978-0-310-27816-0.

Laaser, Mark, and Ralph Earle. (2002). *Pornography Trap*. Kansas City, MO: Beacon Hill Press. ISBN 0-8341-1938-2.

Additional Books by Tim Clinton

Clinton, Tim. (1999). *Before a Bad Goodbye*. Nashville, TN: Word. ISBN 0-8499-3743-4.

Clinton, Tim. Davis, Max. (2014). *Ignite Your Faith*. Shippensburg, PA: Destiny Image. ISBN 0-7684-0493-7.

Clinton, Tim. Davis, Max, and Kingsbury, Karen. (2014). *The Impressionist*. Shippensburg, PA: Destiny Image. ISBN 978-0768404913.

Clinton, Tim, and LaHaye, Tim. (2006). *Turn Your Life Around*. New York, NY: Faith Words. ISBN 978-0-446-57910-0.

Clinton, Tim, and Laaser, Mark. (2010). *The Quick-Reference Guide to Sexuality and Relationship Counseling*. Grand Rapids, MI: Baker Books. ISBN 978-0-8010-7236-9.

Clinton, Tim, and Sibcy, Gary. (2002). *Attachments*. Brentwood, TN: Integrity Publishers. ISBN 1-59145-026-8.

___. (2006). *Why You Do The Things You Do*. Brentwood, TN: Integrity Publishers. ISBN 978-1591454205.

Clinton, Julie. (2009). *10 Things You Aren't Telling Him*. Eugene, Ore: Harvest House. ISBN 978-0-7369-2111-4.

___. (2013). *Bounce Back*. Brentwood, TN: Worthy Publishing. ISBN 978-1-61795-158-9.

Healing Past Hurts

Allender, Dan B. (1990). *The Wounded Heart*. Colorado Springs, CO: Navpress. ISBN 08910-92897.

Bass, Ellen, and Davis, Laura. (1988). *Courage to Heal*. New York, NY: Harper & Row. ISBN 0-06-055105-4.

Langberg, Diane. (1999). *On the Threshold of Hope*. Wheaton, IL: Tyndale House. ISBN 0-8423-4362-8.

Understanding Your Story

Bradshaw, John. (1988). *Healing the Shame That Binds You*. Deerfield Beach, FL: Health Communications. ISBN 0932194869.

___. (1990). *Homecoming*. New York, NY: Bantam Books. ISBN 0-553-35389-6.

Curtis, Brent, and Eldredge, John. (1997). *The Sacred Romance*. Nashville, TN: Thomas Nelson, Inc. ISBN 978-0785273424.

Friel, John and Linda. (1990). *An Adult Child's Guide to What's Normal*. Deerfield Beach, FL: Health Communications, Inc. ISBN 1-55874-090-2.

Smalley, Gary, and John Trent. (1986). *The Blessing*. Nashville, TN: Thomas Nelson. ISBN 0-671-73743-0.

Whitfield, Charles. (1987). *Healing the Child Within*. Deerfield Beach, FL: Health Communications. ISBN 0-932194-40-0.

Wilson, Sandra. (1990). *Released from Shame: Recovery for Adult Children of Dysfunctional Families*. Downers Grove, IL: InterVarsity Press. ISBN 0-8308-1601-1.

SEXUALITY

Carnes, Patrick. (1997). *Sexual Anorexia*. Center City, MN: Hazelden. ISBN 1-56838-144-1.

Ethridge, Shannon, and Thomas, Gary. (2014). *The Passion Principles*. Nashville, TN: W Publishing Group. ISBN 978-0-8499-6447-3.

Gresh, Dannah. (2011). *What Are You Waiting For?* Colorado Springs, Co: WaterBrook Press. ISBN 978-1-60142-331-3.

Maltz, Wendy. (1992). *Sexual Healing Journey*. New York, NY: Harper Perennial. ISBN 0-06-016661-4.

Penner, Cliff and Joyce. (1993). *Restoring the Pleasure*. Dallas, TX: Word. ISBN 0-8499-3464-8.

Rosenau, Doug. (1994). *The Celebration of Sex*. Nashville, TN: Thomas Nelson. ISBN 0-7852-7366-2.

Healing for Couples

Bader, Ellyn, and Pearson, Peter. (1988). *In Quest of the Mythical Mate*. New York, NY: Brunner/Mazel, Inc. ISBN 0-87630-516-8.

Carder, Dave. (1991). *Torn Asunder: Recovering From Extramarital Affairs*. Chicago, IL: Moody Press. ISBN 0-8024-7748-8.

Clinton, Tim. (1999). *Before a Bad Goodbye*. Nashville, TN: Word. ISBN 0-8499-3743-4.

Ferguson, Jen, and Ferguson, Craig. (2014). *Pure Eyes, Clean Heart*. Grand Rapids, MI: RBC Ministries. ISBN 978-1-62707-056-0.

Hendrix, Harville. (1988). *Getting the Love You Want*. New York, NY: Henry Holt and Company. ISBN 0-8050-6895-3.

Thomas, Gary. (2000). *Sacred Marriage*. Grand Rapids, MI: Zondervan. ISBN 0-310-24282-7.

GENERAL RECOVERY AND WELL BEING

Cloud, Henry and Townsend, John. (1992). *Boundaries*. Grand Rapids, MI: Zondervan. ISBN 0-310-58590-2.

___. (1995). *Safe People*. Grand Rapids, MI: Zondervan. ISBN 0-310-21084-4.

___. (2001). How *People Grow*. Grand Rapids, MI: Zondervan. ISBN 0-310-22153-6.

Hart, Archibald. (1995). *Adrenaline and Stress*. Nashville, TN: W Publishing Group. ISBN 0-8499-3690-X.

___. (1999). *The Anxiety Cure*. Nashville, TN: W Publishing Group. ISBN 0-8499-4296-9.

Hart, Archibald, and Hart Weber, Catherine. (2002). *Unveiling Depression in Women*. Grand Rapids, MI: Fleming H. Revell. ISBN 0-8007-5749-1.

Hemfelt, Robert, Minirth, Frank, and Meier, Paul. (1989). *Love Is a Choice*. Nashville, TN: Thomas Nelson. ISBN 0-8407-3189-2.

May, Gerald. (1988). *Addiction and Grace*. New York, NY: Harper. ISBN 0-06-065537-2.

Swenson, Richard. (2004). *Margin: Restoring Emotional, Physical, Financial and Time Reserves to Overloaded Lives*. Colorado Springs, CO: NavPress. ISBN 1-57683-682-7.

TRANSFORMING YOUR BRAIN

Struthers, William. (2009). *Wired for Intimacy.* Downers Grove, IL: Intervarsity Press. ISBN 978-0-8308-3700-7.

Jennings, Timothy R. (2013). *The God-Shaped Brain.* Downers Grove, IL: Intervarsity Press. ISBN 978-0-8308-3416-7.

INSPIRATIONAL

Crabb, Larry. (2001). *Shattered Dreams: God's Unexpected Pathway to Joy.* Colorado Springs, CO: Waterbrook Press. ISBN 1-57856-452-2.

The Journey of Recovery: A New Testament, Colorado Springs, CO: International Bible Society, 2006.

Kendall, R.T. (2002). *Total Forgiveness.* Lake Mary, FL: Charisma House. ISBN 0-06-250589-0.

Kidd, Sue Monk. (1990). *When the Heart Waits.* New York, NY: Harper Collins. ISBN 0-06-064587-3.

Nouwen, Henri. (1994). *The Return of the Prodigal Son.* New York, NY: Image Books. ISBN 0385473071.

___. (1996). *The Inner Voice of Love: A Journey Through Anguish to Freedom.* New York, NY: Image Books. ISBN 0-385-48348-1.

Ortberg, John. (2001). *If You Want to Walk on Water, You've Got to Get Out of the Boat.* Grand Rapids, MI: Zondervan. ISBN 0-310-23927-3.

___. (2003). *Everybody's Normal Till You Get to Know Them.* Grand Rapids, MI: Zondervan. ISBN 0-310-22864-6.

Warren, Rick. (2002). *The Purpose Driven Life.* Grand Rapids, MI: Zondervan. ISBN 0-310-20571-9.

Wilkinson, Bruce. (2003). *The Dream Giver.* Sisters, OR: Multnomah Publishers. ISBN 1-59052-201-X.

Wilson, Sandra D. (1998). *Into Abba's Arms: Finding the Acceptance You've Always Wanted.* Wheaton, IL: Tyndale House Publishers. ISBN 0-8423-2473-9.

FOR FURTHER TRAINING

The American Association of Christian Counselors is the leading training organization for Christian counselors around the world. They have online course- and video-based curriculums in a variety of fields including healthy sexuality and sexual addiction. They also offer certification for those pastors, counselors, and therapists who may be interested in gaining greater competence in working with those who are sexually addicted. For more information, we invite you to visit the AACC website (aacc.net) and Light University (LightUniversity.com).

ABOUT THE AUTHORS

TIM CLINTON, EdD, is President of the nearly 50,000-member American Association of Christian Counselors (AACC), the largest and most diverse Christian counseling association in the world. He is Professor of Counseling and Pastoral Care, and Executive Director of the Center for Counseling and Family Studies at Liberty University. Licensed in Virginia as both a Professional Counselor (LPC) and Marriage and Family Therapist (LMFT), Tim now spends a majority of his time working with Christian leaders and professional athletes. He is recognized as a world leader in faith and mental health issues and has authored over 20 books including *Breakthrough: When to Give In, When to Push Back.* Most importantly, Tim has been married 33 years to his wife Julie and together they have two children, Megan (recently married to Ben Allison) and Zach. For more information, visit www.TimClinton.com and www.AACC.net.

MARK LAASER, MDiv, PhD, is the Founder and President of Faithful & True, a Christian-based counseling center in Eden Prairie, Minnesota, specializing in the treatment of sexual addiction and relational betrayal. Dr. Laaser is nationally regarded as the leading Christian authority in the field of sexual health and addiction and has authored a dozen books on the subject, including *Healing The Wounds of Sexual Addiction,* and his 3-book *Men of Valor* series. Mark and his wife, Debbie Laaser, MA, LMFT, have helped thousands of men and women achieve healing and restoration to their marriages through their counseling work at Faithful & True. They are also the authors of their highly acclaimed book, *The Seven Desires of Every Heart* (Zondervan Publishing).

Mark is also the host of *The Men of Valor Program,* Faithful & True's weekly online radio show. He holds a PhD degree from the University of Iowa and a divinity degree from Princeton Theological Seminary. Mark and Debbie are the proud parents of three grown children and live in Chanhassen, Minnesota.

Contact: Dr. Mark Laaser, Faithful & True, 15798 Venture Lane, Eden Prairie, MN 55344, Phone: 952-746-3880, Email: info@faithfulandtrue.com, Web: www.faithfulandtrue.com.